COINCIDENCE OR CHRIST?

COINCIDENCE OR CHRIST?

The Edgewood Story

BY DR. JOHN W. LYND

To the Christian, life's incidents are no coincidence.

TABLE OF CONTENTS

PREFACE AND INTRODUCTION

INTRODUCTION

Without the vision of Juvenile Judge Arthur Yergey and the call of God upon Pastor Tom Wenig and the program of Jack Lynd, the Edgewood Children's Ranch would never have had its genesis in 1966.

While I cannot speak for Judge Yergey or Pastor Tom Wenig, I can give my own reflections taken from notes, newspaper articles, and my daily calendars, over a period of twenty-two years.

The following story is as I remember it.

My sincere thanks to hundreds of individuals, groups, churches, grocery stores and others too numerous to mention, for their participation.

But the Ranch could not have succeeded without God's calling upon the following to name just a few:

Dr. Joan Consolver My right hand for twenty years; loyal, tireless, uplifting, and patient. After my retirement she has directed the Ranch, never diverting from the original program for the past twenty-four years. At the award ceremony with

Jesus, I believe that she has several "crowns" for her works in gold, silver and bronze. She is quite a Christian Lady.

John Lynd, Jr. At the beginning he was all I had at times to supervise the boys while I was away making speeches. As an eighteen-year-old, supervising boys ages fourteen to sixteen, this was quite an accomplishment. He often reminded me that his only pay was an old black-and-white TV (that didn't work).

Bob Butterfield Chairman of the Board for nineteen years, and my daily source of support. He helped me in decisions regarding integration, becoming co-ed, raising money for payroll, and other necessities. He was instrumental in our long fight with HRS in getting out from under state control, and a real champion for Christ.

George Bailey Publisher of the *Winter Garden Times*. He never failed to keep the public informed regarding the Ranch and her activities. He was a good and loyal friend.

So many others The Colburns ("Leisure and Bill"), Don Phillips, John Pattillo, Wally Sanderlin, Walker Miller, Dr. Don Brown and many others.

And of course my wife **Ruth**, who was by my side through it all.

In order to see the values and understand the concept of this information, it will first be necessary to give a capsule background on Juvenile Delinquency and the way that it has been handled in the past.

Juvenile Delinquency and crime are as old as man. In Genesis 4:8 we read, "Cain rose up against Abel his brother and slew Him." Ancient Egypt has recorded in hieroglyphics, "The times are out of joint, children do not obey their elders." History has recorded crime against society since the beginning of time.

The first specialized institution for children can be traced back to 1704 in Rome, where a center "for the correction and instruction of indigent youth" was established. Similar institutions were established in Germany and other countries during the first half of the nineteenth century.

A school for the children of adult criminals was established in London in 1788 and during the early nineteenth century, schools were founded for neglected children. The Kingswood Reformatory was established in 1852 for "unruly children" who infested the streets of the new industrial towns of England.

The evolution of "The Training School" began in America in 1825. Prior to this time there were no separate institutions for Juvenile Offenders. The first separate institution for homeless children, which marked the beginning of removal of children for alms housed, was established in New Orleans, Louisiana in 1727. Most of our states continued to place boys and girls convicted of offenses in jails and prison, right along with adult offenders.

The first separate institutions for juvenile offenders in this country was, "The New York House of Refuge" and was opened in 1825 by a private society. Boston followed suit in 1828, although its first facility was a portion of a building used to house adult offenders.

In the sixteenth century, America's uncared-for children were "indentured" or "bound-out." One such account was dated in 1636:"

> "The first child placed out by public authority was Benjamin Eaton. He was indentured in 1636 by the governor and assistants of Plymouth Colony to Bridget Fuller, a widow for fourteen years, she was to keep him in school two years and to employ him after in such service as she saw good and that he should be fit for; but not to turn him over to any other without the governor's consent."

As an accepted child-care practice, it was natural that indenture became an early part of the programs of institutions for juvenile offenders. The Daily Journal kept by the superintendent of the New York House of Refuge reported under the date of May 10, 1828: "We saw the eight boys for Ohio start in good spirits.... It excited considerable good feelings to see so many little fellows bound for such a good and suitable place from the House of Refuge, among the passengers on board the steamboat."

In 1893, a Homer Folks began to advocate foster homes for delinquents and urged that "only the very small number who show lack of moral sense and are dangerous to the community be sent to Institutions."

In 1860, The Boston Aid Society began a new concept by the initiation of "Probation." This allowed offenders to stay in their own homes and communities. In 1890 the first Juvenile Courts were organized, bringing into focus the changing public attitude toward delinquent children.

Institutions at this time were largely located in urban areas and as population expanded were required, by their very nature, to provide fences and isolate the children. This necessitated a move toward rural settings where large acreages were acquired for farming and agriculture purposes. This was the beginning of what is known as "The Colony System."

In the latter part of the nineteenth century, emphasis was placed upon trade or vocational training and many of the schools now changed their names to Industrial Schools from the formerly used "Reform Schools."

The Boys Industrial School, at Lancaster, Ohio, opened in 1856 and introduced "The Cottage System," a system used in most Training Schools today.

As World War I approached, the Industrial Schools became military-oriented and cottages became "companies," living units, barracks, and superintendents carried the title of "Colonel." Some Training Schools today still utilize this type of training; however, modern knowledge does not support it.

The widespread introduction of psychiatry following World War I had its impact on Training Schools in the 1920s. The Social Security Act of 1935 provided much needed "home care" and helped cut Training School population.

In 1958, there were some two hundred Training Schools in the fifty states, District of Columbia, Puerto Rico, and the Virgin Islands. During 1959, these Institutions had a combined daily population of about 40,000 boys and girls.

I would like to say a few words with reference to the punitive type of rehabilitation versus treatment. Prior to 1940, very little was done in Training Schools with reference to treatment. Discipline was harsh and brutal, and many of the schools used a leather strap about three feet long to beat the kids into submission and to teach them the mistake of mal-behavior. I believe that this method of discipline simply drives the hostility deeper into the child, which will express itself in some other form of mal-behavior or "acting-out" at a later time.

At the Boys Industrial School in Ohio the change-over from punitive treatment was initiated in May 1959. I headed up the department that was to replace the former Disciplinarian.

Before talk about treatment, let me take a few minutes to explain the procedures for punishment under the punitive method of rehabilitation.

If a lad got into some kind of trouble at his Cottage, on his work job, or at school, recreation, or military drill, the report was written on a "blue-slip." He was then escorted to the Discipline Cottage where the Disciplinarian had his office. He was usually escorted by the officer who initiated the report or by a couple of "hoods" who acted as monitors. Here he would face the Disciplinarian, who would read the charges and then pronounce sentence. The boy was always guilty, no matter what had happened. The usual penalty was confinement in the Discipline Cottage for a specified number of days, with or without the added penalty of a "strapping." A whipping consisted of from five licks or more with the "strap" and was severe enough to make the child scream.

The Discipline Cottage was staffed by punitive-minded employees who got a perverse kick out of punishing the boys in any derogatory manner that they could conceive. They were aided by monitors, usually big, tough boys capable of beating up the other inmates. For the slightest infraction of unrealistic rules, a boy would be placed "on line." This consisted of the boy standing with his face and toes flat against the wall for hours at a time. It was determined that this type of care did not cut down the rate of mal-behavior.

To reiterate, in May 1959, a new department opened of which I was supervisor. It was called the Reception and Adjustment Department, and it initiated the treatment phase at the school. As opposed to the former system, all reports of incidents were processed through an Adjustment Committee, which reviewed the report to see if it was consistent with good treatment practices. All employees were checked to see if they were following policy. The boy reported was allowed to state in writing whether or not the report was true. Where there was reasonable doubt as to the truth of validity of a report, it was thoroughly checked out. This department also had charge of a new facility called the Annex Cottage, which took the place of the Discipline Cottage. The Annex was treatment-oriented with Social Workers on duty at all times. All boys domiciled there were tested by the psychologist and, if needed, were referred to the psychiatrist. Plans were then made for each boy, treating each case individually; giving him a definite program for the remainder of his stay at the school. In other words, the school went from one extreme to the other. Just as in the boy's home, where discipline would vacillate from brutal authoritarianism to extreme permissiveness, the school did the same thing.

After seven years as a department head, I came to the conclusion that we were no closer to success under the so-called treatment system than we had been under the punitive approach. Boys were still recidivating at a fifty percent rate. This means that on a national average, that one out of two boys sent to a State Training School would get into further trouble with the law.

During the past several years, were spent many idle hours thinking about what, if anything, could be done to help the delinquent boy. We realized that as there was no single cause for delinquency, there could be no single cure. The program must start with the entire family constellation. There must be a sincere desire to want to change from the life of discord to something better. There must be a basic faith in order to have a beginning. There must be a discipline established to train the boy and his family to meet a competitive society in later years. Most important of all, they must be taught to love instead of hate.

The mushrooming problem of Juvenile Delinquency has been described a society's time-bomb. It is one of America's foremost moral and social problems. It strikes in homes of all walks of life, income, and area. All children, whether they are in your home, on your block, or in your community are potential delinquents. This is true of any child who has problems too complex for him to solve. Neighborhood gangs take the place of the family.

Never before in the history of our country have our children been subjected to so much stress and strain. Their disturbance in complexity far exceeds that of any other generation.

This dilemma has greatly excited many responsible Orange County citizens, and they have decided to do something about it. It is their feeling that it is essential a movement be initiated to establish a domiciliary wholly supported by local citizenry, where our local children might be retrained. The cost of the project has been placed squarely upon the shoulders and hearts of the people of our area who are concerned enough with the delinquency problem to help financially and materially. But then, how do you figure the cost of a program such as this? How do you figure the cost to a family whose father has been shot down in cold blood by a hostile young juvenile in a robbery attempt? How do you figure the cost of emotional and physical damage to a young girl who was raped by one of a group of young hoodlums, or the cost to a young boy and his family who was sexually assaulted and murdered? This happened in Pompano Beach, by a delinquent boy returned from Marianna, where he had been sent one and half years before for the same offense, and had been released as rehabilitated.

Forty-two years ago, a group of Orange County Christian business and professional men sat down to talk about this problem and what they could do about it. Among the men was D. Arthur Yergey, a Juvenile Judge. He explained to the gentlemen that at the time, the court had only two courses open to it, with reference to disposition of youngsters appearing before it: (1) Direct commitment of the child to the State Training School at Marianna. (2) Return the child home under the guidance of one of the Court Counselors.

This first recourse had been used in the past only for the more sophisticated delinquent who it was felt could not profit by a counseling situation in the home. A boy usually goes to the State Training School as an amateur law-breaker. He will in many cases, return a sophisticated delinquent capable of committing a large range of crimes, due to the education he received from peers while at the school. As previously stated, national statistics indicate that one out of two boys sent to a State Training School, on a national average, will get into further trouble with the law. This is not necessarily the fault of school officials or staff. Actually, they should be commended for the excellent job they perform in view of staff shortages, lack of monies, outside pressures, political pressures, and more. However, this is not a desirable situation.

The second recourse was sending the boy home to the same environment that had contributed, in many cases to his delinquencies. Sending him home to a family who were at a loss on how to handle the boy, or who, for one reason or the other simply did not care. This was even less desirable.

The question now raised was, "Okay, we want to help. How will we go about it?" In the past, millions and millions of dollars have been spent in an attempt to cure delinquency. Government grants, state and local monies, and private foundations have all advanced money for the various concepts, with the hope of finding a cure. None up to this time have proven successful. As we looked at various concepts that advanced, we noted that they invariably treated delinquency as a condition of emotions, or a condition of the body. They attempted to affect the cure through psychiatric or medical help. It was apparent that with the continued rise in Juvenile Delinquency, this wasn't the answer. From this thought developed a new concept. Since delinquency is opposed to law and order, it is also opposed to God's laws, and thus by its very nature becomes a condition of the soul. The only power that can cure a soul-sickness is Jesus Christ. Therefore, the entire plan must be predicated upon a belief in God and a willingness on the part of the boy and his family to want to experience a change in their lives. They must want a better life than the one of discord that they have been leading. They must express that they will return to the church of their choice and begin to live a life adhering to Christian principles.

The question then arose with reference to the Jewish boy. How would he fit into a Christian-oriented rehabilitation unit? It was noted that if we had to set up units to rehabilitate the Jewish boy, we would not have a delinquency problem. We could all learn from the Jewish people, as they take care of their own. However, if the occasion should arise, we would take the Jewish boy and turn his spiritual training over to the Rabbi of his choice.

Now with this concept established, the men incorporated the new non-profit organization under the name of "The Edgewood Boys Ranch Foundation, Inc."

On July 31, 1966, Judge Yergey cut the ribbon at a formal opening ceremony. On August 15, the first two boys were brought to the Ranch.

The following is a capsule of Court procedure and the program at the Ranch, and with the family in the community.

Each boy is given a Court hearing at which time both he and his parents express a desire to utilize the opportunity at the Ranch. He is then given a suspended commitment to the State Training School and is committed to the Edgewood Boys Ranch. (Later, this procedure was accomplished with a conference at the ranch, where his parents agreed to participate in the program.) He is then placed with Christian adults in a highly moral, family type environment. It is the purpose of the Ranch to bring up the boy in a Christian environment, and to provide him with Christian principles on which to live his life.

Children learn of God through human experiences. They are born with a child-like faith but due to traumatic experiences, lose this faith over the years. How can a boy trust a heavenly father whom he can't see, if he cannot trust an earthly father he can see? Many of the kids have "lost faith in people." They are disillusioned.

The purpose of the Ranch is a redemptive one. It initially must restore faith in the boy. This easily breaks into faith in self, faith in others, and faith in his peer group. He asks himself the question, "What is wrong with me? Why am I different?" The problem usually lies in adults and it takes much love and care to restore that faith, both in self and in others. Only then can the knowledge of a loving and forgiving God be accepted and a personal relationship take place.

The Cottage Parents are kind, sympathetic, and understanding but firm with reference to the rules. It has been experienced that most delinquents come from homes where the discipline vacillates between brutal authoritarianism and extreme permissiveness. There is no mean established. At the Ranch there are limits set for the boy. He is allowed to test these limits as often as he cares to, but the minute he exceeds them, he is chastised. Chastisement consists of removal of privileges, such as attendance at football games, social functions, and TV privileges. If the infraction occurs frequently enough or is of serious nature, the boy is paddled. The Executive Director handles the more punitive types of punishment, because this sometimes will bring out a sadistic instinct on the part of untrained Cottage Parents.

It is also felt that a distinction must be made between rights and privileges. For example, it is the child's right to visit with his parents, to have warm and suitable clothing, a clean bed, proper food, and love and understanding from the staff. Privileges include social activities, recreation, fishing, hunting, TV, and dating. We will never deny a child his rights.

While the child is domiciled at the Ranch they receive daily family worship periods at which time the Bible is read. The children are allowed discussions with reference to the reading, and are encouraged to arrive at their own conclusions. They attend Church Services on Sunday afternoon. On Sunday evening and on Wednesday evening, we have an extended family worship period. Different lay people from the various recognized denominations handle our services on other evenings.

There is a strong recreational and physical therapy program that begins with calisthenics at 6:15 a.m. The children also participate in weightlifting, all the water sports, group games, boxing, wrestling, arts and crafts, and other activities. They must have healthy bodies to go along with their healthy minds.

Much stress is placed upon their formal academic schooling. Most children in this class are academically retarded at least one year. There is a study period of one hour each evening for their homework or for extra credit. Tutors from the community work with the children in their weak areas.

The children's social life consists of school activities, such as scouting, bar-b-ques, and Sunday School groups. Each child is shown socially acceptable means of having fun, as opposed to his former life of discord. On October 23, 1966, there was established what we feel was a first for organizations like Edgewood Boy's Ranch. The St. Andrews Presbyterian Church took our entire complement of boys into their individual homes for a weekend of fun and recreation, as well as exposing them to the life available to a child who has and uses Christian principles. This has been continued throughout the years, utilizing many different Christian families in the community.

Each child is also given a work experience to prepare him for his future labors in later life. He is taught how to make his bed, sew on buttons, make minor clothing repairs, iron, wash dishes, housekeeping duties, and personal and oral hygiene. He learns how to make minor repairs around the house and on the equipment, how and when to plant flowers, and how to take care of a garden. He is obligated to spend a specified amount of hours each week in labor.

These are the basic concepts for the re-training of the child while he is at the Ranch:

1. A deep spiritual experience with the hope that he will learn to place his trust in God's Son, Jesus Christ, and to lean on Him when he needs reassurance or guidance.
2. A strong recreational program to build a strong, healthy body to go with his new and different life.
3. An accelerated academic program with properly developed study habits to build a strong and analytical mind.
4. To provide a different social life to equip them with socially acceptable methods of meeting with and dealing with the public.
5. To provide them with a work experience that will discipline them for their life-labors ahead.

At this point you are probably saying to yourself, "What makes this program unique? Hasn't this been tried before? There is no such thing as a delinquent child, only delinquent parents." The Ranch's concept will also handle this problem. It involves the entire family constellation, and that is what makes it unique.

The Ranch begins to process the child to return home when those concerned feel that the family has progressed satisfactorily and is ready to assume the responsibility with reference to the child. They have been made cognizant of their behavioral pattern and how to cope with it, should it arise in the future.

Again for the first time, to the Ranch's knowledge, a child will not return to the same environment that has contributed, in many cases, to his delinquencies. Instead he will return to a continuance of the type of life that he had been leading, a new life, law-abiding, and socially acceptable.

The first Ranch was opened on faith. It was started with thirty dollars, and God has seen fit to provide the Ranch with enough to meet its needs. The Ranch is totally dependent upon those individuals, churches, clubs and organizations who are concerned enough with the delinquency problem to give financial and material support.

CHAPTER ONE
BEGINNING

Testimony of Starting the Ranch

With $30.000, two boys and a rented house—what to do? Jesus said, "Go unto all the world; tell them of me." So without any other resource than the belief in Jesus' power to provide, we set out. We made over 500 speeches to community charities, groups, and clubs. We explained our program and what Jesus was doing at the Ranch and they began to visit.

Each visiting person saw young boys, supposedly delinquent, with a smile on their faces, extremely courteous, and they normally asked, "What is this child doing here?" They saw a tremendous need, such as food, clothing, furniture, tools, equipment, and cleaning supplies. On subsequent visits, they began to supply all of these needs. They would bring food and even prepare it. They got clothing sizes and provided clothing. School supplies were furnished. Some people realized that children needed pets. So they brought out dogs, cats, sheep, turkeys pigs, horses, ponies, a bull, goldfish, rabbits, and food for these creatures. Most of all they sent money. Salaries, utility bills, insurance, and gasoline all needed to be paid. There was never enough money to pay the accumulated bills, but every one got paid. (Elisha and the widow woman and the cruise of oil).

We spoke at churches of all denominations. We aren't speaking regarding doctrine, but salvation. We preached, spoke to women's groups, men's groups, and children. We taught Sunday School, spoke at church banquets, Easter Sunrise Services or wherever they would let us speak, always on the providing power of our Lord Jesus Christ. These groups visited us and became involved. We spoke to Rotary Clubs, Civitan, Optimist, Kiwanis, Masonic Lodges, and Chambers of Commerce in our tri-county area. They all came and brought support. We spoke to groups of Motorcycle Clubs, skeptics and unbelievers who also came to visit and were witnessed to by our children. They loved to tell others of what Christ had done for them and their families.

When a child first came to the ranch, at the initial interview with his parents, they were told that the Ranch was a Christian facility. They were told of the plan of salvation, and thousands have prayed for Christ to come into their hearts and save them at this initial meeting. Thousands of lives have been changed.

The children were told, "You have been living the life of turmoil, unhappiness, and disobedience to your parents, school authorities and civil authorities. You have been unhappy and really wanted what you have seen in more successful people, but you didn't know how to achieve this."

"Jesus has now come into your hearts. You have received the new birth. *You are a new person*. You now belong to the family of God. God is your "Heavenly Father" and is now responsible for your welfare. You talk with Him in prayer and He always answers. As a member of His family you cannot go to hell. Your future is with Jesus in Heaven. So forget all the bad things in your life and being this new life with a clean conscience, a positive attitude and the knowledge that you are now indwelt by God, the Holy Spirit, and He will guide you throughout the rest of your life on Earth. Congratulations you are now a child, a prince or princess of the King."

Parents have to agree to attend weekly parenting services where they are taught how to have a Christian home. They too have been saved and now need to live a Christian life. The children are sent home one weekend a month and during Easter and Christmas breaks. The parents are then asked how the child behaved in the home. The children are counseled as to how the parents were doing in their Christian walk. All the negatives were then handled as we walked through existing problems. Sometimes it took months or even years, but once the family was living a Christian harmonious life, we reunited the family.

We used different ways to settle children down in this, their first absence from home. Each cottage had a pet and sometimes we would see a child sitting with his or her arms wrapped around a little puppy dog. Crying as if their heart was broke, the little dog would look at them with perfect understanding, and with tears in its own eyes.

Each cottage had a fireplace and fish tank. Looking at fire or water will settle a person down. (Also an analogy of God's wrath in the flood and the coming tribulation.)

The children have a daily routine that they follow. When they arise in the morning, they sing a hymn of their choice as they make their bunks, put dirty clothes in the washer, and clean their house. (Each cottage has a clothesline outside and these are used instead of dryers, due to the high cost of electricity. Some of the little guys have to use a small stool to stand on to hang up their clothes (really a heart-tugging sight). The family then meets for devotion and prayer. Afterward it's off to breakfast in the dining hall, and then to our on-campus school.

CHAPTER TWO

COINCIDENCE OR CHRIST?

One day I was making a speech to a local Rotary Club. After I finished telling of the miracles of answered prayers, a man in the audience said, "These are not miracles but coincidences." I thought that I ought to write about a few of the "things" that have happened at the Edgewood Children's Ranch and let the reader decide. Are these things that would have happened anyway, or are they caused by the direct intervention of our Lord Jesus Christ as the answer to prayer?

The Edgewood Children's Ranch had a very inauspicious beginning. We began with two boys, thirty dollars, and faith that God would meet our needs.

The need for the Ranch was established by the local Juvenile Court Judge when he would have a child appear before him for an act of delinquency and he only had two courses open to him. One was direct commitment to the State Training School and the other to return the child home, under the direction of a Juvenile Court Counselor.

The first recourse was used for the more sophisticated delinquent whom the judge felt could not profit by a counseling situation in the home. A boy usually was sent to the Training

School as an amateur lawbreaker but in many cases, returned as a potential career criminal due to the education he received from peers while at the school. National statistics at the time indicated a 50 percent recidivism rate.

The second recourse was to send the child home under the supervision of a Court Counselor. This was even less desirable than the reform school commitment because the child simply had his wrist slapped and thought it was all a big joke.

We decided to start a local facility where these children could be retrained. We felt that the cause of the problem was due to the breakdown of the basic unit in our society—the FAMILY.

The typical Edgewood child is a child for whom life came without a safety net. His enrollment may have been precipitated by a unique event, but there is an underlying pattern to his life, which holds true for almost every student.

The pattern is this:

1. The home is under stress for one or more of these reasons:
   - A. Divorce
   - B. Alcohol or drug abuse
   - C. Child abuse

2. As a result of the stressful home environment, the child has:
   - A. Failed in school
   - B. Caused problems in society.

Since he has not yet become a ward of the state, the child comes to Edgewood by his own choice, usually at the strong suggestion of school authorities. In choosing to enroll, he agrees to accept the discipline of the facility, which includes: work, athletics, study, and religious instruction. In addition, the parent(s) agree to attend chapel with the child and participate in family counseling.

The Edgewood program is not unlike that of other Christian boarding schools, except that students are accepted on the basis of need and the desire to participate rather than the ability to pay. Parents contribute what they feel they can. The balance is made up by the generosity of the community, which contributes "in-kind" and in volunteer hours as well as monetarily. In 1975, it cost less than thirty dollars per day to school and house a child at Edgewood, since food was provided by local grocers.

Edgewood does not keep a child past the time that the family is sufficiently stable to re-accept him and/or the child is willing and able to function at the grade level appropriate to his age.

The work program at Edgewood consists of housework, including laundry, necessary to maintain the home in which ten children live with house parents. There are nine homes, or cottages, on the Edgewood campus. Lawn care, rotating K.P. in the central kitchen and light maintenance in the small citrus grove complete the chores. Girls sometimes assist in the office or answer the phone. In addition, the goats, cats, horse, and other animals that call Edgewood home must be fed and groomed.

Athletic activities are intramural and include football, soccer, basketball, softball, wrestling, track, and water sports. There is a golf driving range on campus where visiting pros sometimes hold clinics.

The Edgewood School uses the non-graded Accelerated Christian Education (A.C.E.) curriculum, which is recognized by the State of Florida. A formula exists whereby a transition can be made by A.C.E. students into the public school program. When a child enrolls at Edgewood, he is given a battery of tests to determine what level he can function in each subject. (It would not be unusual to find a fifteen-year-old non-reader who worked at the third grade level in math). The student is assigned a workbook in each subject, according to his current proficiency. He works at his own pace with one-on-one instruction as necessary, and may cover as much material as he can master. He is encouraged by liberal praise and the positive peer pressure that is developed in each home by older students and cottage parents. It is not unusual for a student to cover two (or sometimes more) grades in one year. All teachers are certified and are assisted by community volunteers who are often retired teachers themselves.

Ethics and patriotism are integrated into all subjects wherever possible. Old-fashioned manners are taught and practiced.

Bible is taught in school and chapel, but sectarianism is not practiced. Even in doctrine as basic as baptism, Edgewood refers the candidate to the church of his or his parents' choice. The current staff and volunteer helpers include members of most denominations.

Duty to God and country coupled with a determination to make the most of one's natural talents are the attitudes Edgewood seeks to foster in each of its children.

We began to look for a place where we could begin this venture and found a large house on Pine Island Lake in Lake County. We were able to get a year's lease with the option to renew for another year. One of the members of the Board of Trustees paid the initial $175 monthly payment. With the two boys and faith that God would bless us, we prayed for our supper that first day and two ladies brought us a meal. We haven't missed a meal in twenty-two years.

Our plan was to give our Ranch to our Heavenly Father and then depend solely upon Him for our needs. We had family devotions each night where we would read from the scripture and then discuss it. We stayed away from doctrinal discussions and were concerned with each child accepting Jesus Christ as his personal savior, knowing that the Holy Spirit would lead him in these other areas. We would then get down on our knees and have our open prayer. We prayed to our Heavenly Father in Jesus name, believing and knowing that God would answer our prayers.

One of the ways that Christ has revealed Himself through the Ranch can be shown as follows:

We had a young man come to us who had been found guilty of breaking and entering at a local Holiday Inn. His father had married a young eighteen-year-old girl and could not share his love with his son. The father, step-mother and the boy were riding the dad's motorcycle one day when the step-mother shoved the boy off the back of the motorcycle and she and the father laughed at him. He was totally humiliated as he sat in the middle of the street. They circled around, came back to pick him up, and then went back home. He ran away from home that night and broke into the Holiday Inn in Orlando. The lad had been at the Ranch for about ten months and he prayed continually that his father might some day come back to see him. One night when we were on our knees praying, and this particular boy was praying about his dad, the phone began to ring. We tried to ignore it but it kept on ringing. Finally I got up and went to the phone and answered it. It was the boy's dad.

He told me he was in Georgia and had finally realized what he had done. We made arrangements for him to see his son the following day.

Was this just coincidence or was this the work of Jesus Christ?

We had another boy at this same time who we'll call Joe. Let me tell you about Joe.

Joe was from a very wealthy family. His grandmother was on drugs, his mother was an alcoholic, and his father had abandoned him when he was only six-months-old. Joe had been at a military school when his mother visited him one day. She was drunk and wearing a bikini. She embarrassed him so badly that he ran away and ended up at the Ranch. Joe saw that his Ranch brother's dad came back, and he asked, "If I pray, will I get to see my daddy some day?" I really felt like a hypocrite when I told him, "Son, if you pray to your Heavenly Father in Christ's name and believe you will get to see your dad, it will happen." I felt like a hypocrite because we didn't know where his dad was, whether he was alive or dead, where he lived or anything about him. The boy prayed that he might one day see his dad. One day a man walked into my office and asked to see his son. One look into his face told me that it was Joe's dad. He came to Florida from Connecticut to search out his son that he had abandoned fifteen-and-one-half years before.

Could this be coincidental or did Christ touch a heart, after all these years, to answer a young man's prayer?

We had another youngster who was assigned to the Ranch because of his hostility toward his step-mother. He refused to obey her or his natural father and was adjudicated an incorrigible child. Because of the new routine of daily living as a Christian, he invited Jesus into his heart and became a Christian. Several weeks after his release home, he was working on his dad's used car lot when a young couple approached him about buying a car. They were cursing and he asked them if they knew Christ. They answered, "No." The lad was scared to continue and he forgot what to say. Then he remembered Romans 10:9, "If thou shalt confess with thy mouth the Lord Jesus, and shalt believe in thine heart that God hath raised him from the dead, thou shalt be saved." He was able to lead the young lady to Christ.

Could coincidence have placed these three people in this improbable circumstance, or did Jesus Christ arrange this divine appointment?

We were called into juvenile court one day and found the following scene:

A drunken father with vomit on his clothing, a nineteen-year-old daughter who had moved out of the family home due to the condition of the father, and a sixteen-year-old son who had been picked up for shoplifting at Ivey's in Winter Park. The boy was committed to the Ranch.

The day following the court hearings, juvenile court chaplains, along with the Associate Minister of the First Methodist Church of Orlando, visited the father. The father dropped to his knees and asked God to give him the strength to stop drinking so that he might gain his family back. Some five months later, picture this scene:

The same courtroom, the father in a clean suit, shirt, tie, shoes shined, and sober. The daughter having moved back into the house, seemingly at peace with the world and the son, who had spent the second semester on the honor roll at the local school, being returned to the family.

This family had been completely separated from God, and the Ranch personnel and chaplains were able to reconcile them to their Heavenly Father. The postscript to this story is that the boy graduated from college, the girl married and has a family, and the father is still "on the wagon."

We feel that the cause of all the problems in our society is due to the breakdown of the basic unit in our society, the family. We feel that the family unit has broken down because it has become separated from God. We know that the only way to correct this national problem is to bring this basic unit, the family, back into a right relationship with God. Therefore, before we will accept a child at the Edgewood Ranch, his parents, or parent, must agree to work with us as we attempt to work through their problems. There is no point in retraining a child and returning him to the same environment that contributed to his misbehavior. We insist upon their attendance at our Ranch Church services. I have heard parents say, "You can't make us accept Jesus Christ." Our answer is, "You're right, but we can put you in a position where you are going to hear about Him."

We have a routine of daily living, as a Christian, at the Ranch and our kids get used to living this way. We want them to continue this routine when they get home, so we try to have the parents change their lifestyle somewhat. We ask that they have family devotions each day, and after devotions they all pray. They have to furnish us with a home church and pastor's name before we will suggest that the child be returned home. We follow through and see that they continue attending church after the child is replaced with the family, as much as we are able.

The following is a letter from a parent whose son was staying at the Ranch when the letter was written:

Dear Mr. Lynd:

We would like very much for you to consider sending our son back home to us; and if you feel that he is ready, that you will take the necessary steps for us to have him as soon as possible. You see, we need this boy as much as he needs his parents and his family. There is just an emptiness in our hearts when we see his empty place at the table and the empty bed in his room each night I or his father check to see if they are too warm or too cold. These past eight months I remembered the many times I had brushed his hair back from his forehead and asked God to help him because I didn't know how. We feel that God has answered our prayers because he was accepted at the Edgewood Ranch.

Our first talk with you was very bewildering because you have such faith, and after an hour of conversation, the same advice kept coming from you: pray, have faith and everything will be fine. That day there seemed to be a complete change, not only in the immediate family but in everyone we were closest to, friends, neighbors and relatives.

The Ranch has taught Paul not to be ashamed of his faith in God and prayer as so many young people are today, and he never fails to witness when the chance arrives. He seems to look forward and enjoys going to church and confirmation. He even asked our Pastor when he could start class before we even had the opportunity. Today the announcement of new classes was made. This is a boy who used to run and hide in the wooded area near us, in order to miss church and Sunday school and declared that no one would ever get him to a confirmation class. We could never leave money or any type of jewelry around the house because he would take it, and he never seemed to care if his brother or sister was blamed or punished. Now he never touches anything that doesn't belong to him without asking.

He does so many helpful things when he's home for a visit without being told, and also the things that we ask him to do. Sometimes he doesn't do them right away but he will do them. In the past he has broken the lawn mower to keep from mowing when it was his turn; now he will repair or adjust it so he can cut the grass. He thought that we were supposed to give him all the money he wanted, and to buy everything he wanted as soon as he asked. He was pretty hard to live with if we refused. He would even hurt his little brother to get back at us. Now he doesn't demand or never asks for money, and will get jobs to make some extra money. He then gets us to save it for him until he comes home. He never fails to buy something for his little brother, if only a sucker.

He is much more gentle with the little one and helps with things he wants to do. We know we can depend on him to help us guide him in the right way because we have heard Paul say to him, "You will do what mother and dad tells you to." Paul's father has learned, since we were a Ranch family, that you do hug your boys as well as your girls; even the eighteen-year-old boy, when he left for the service, and when he came home on leave. Now he writes in his letters to us that he loves dad. He has never written that before when he was away.

As his mother, I have learned to kneel and pray with my children, to thank God for our experience and for everyone at the Ranch. I pray for people I never thought to pray for before, and I feel the need to help people who need help.

We have noticed a sparkle in our twenty-year-old daughter's eyes just over watching her dad hurrying on Sunday morning to get ready for early church. She had asked him so many times to go with us in the past, but he always has a reason for not going, except for the baptism of our children. We have only missed three church services in the eight months that Paul has been at the Ranch.

Both of us are so grateful for the help you have given us, not only with Paul, but advice that has helped us in ways to have a happier, more understanding home life.

Could the reuniting of this family just be coincidental?

One day we received a call from the juvenile judge. He asked that we take a twelve-year-old boy whose mother had been sent to prison. She was sent to prison for stealing and had a sentence of from three to ten years. She had been there for eighteen months, and it was our understanding that she couldn't be paroled for another eighteen months. We accepted the little lad. The day after he arrived he was in the yard crying. His dad had recently died and the lad felt completely alone.

One of his Ranch brothers, a ten-year-old, went over to him, put his arm around his shoulder and said, "Don't cry—let's go pray." In our little chapel, the cottage parents observed the children down on their knees for about fifteen minutes. They got up and walked out of the chapel with smiles on their faces and their arms around each other's shoulder. The next day we received a letter from Lowell Prison, stating that the mother was being paroled the following Monday. We had the pleasure of watching the little fellow climb up on his mother's lap the following week. Coincidental? At the time that the boy was on his knees praying, the prison authorities were putting the parole process in motion for his mother.

The ten-year-old boy who suggested that he and his new brother pray about his situation had been sent to the Ranch as a result of his being a problem in school. His teacher had spanked him, pointed her finger at him and scolded him. He calmly reached up and broke her finger.

We have no budget at the Ranch. We pray for our needs, and God sends them to us. We now serve several hundred thousand meals each year at no dollar expenditure. Several years ago our cottage parents did the cooking. Back in 1969, on February 28, we hired a new cottage couple. That date fell on Friday. The following Monday, they approached me and told me that they needed some cornmeal. I apologized to them for not explaining our method of requisitioning and told them that they didn't ask me for such things; they placed their order with the Lord. They went back to the cottage and prayed. The next day they came down to the office before we arrived and found a twenty-five-pound sack of cornmeal on the steps. We still don't know who brought it, but we do know who sent it.

Another day the cottage dad come into the office telling me that we were out of margarine, mayonnaise, Crisco and ketchup. He had been praying and nothing happened. While we were talking, a car drove up and some ladies from a sorority told us that they had some things for the boys. Included was margarine, mayonnaise, Crisco and ketchup. The cottage dad cried unashamedly.

We allow our children to go home with their families one weekend a month. When they return, we talk to the parents as to how the child behaved during the visit. Did he assume his responsibility as a member of the family? Where was he weak and where was he strong? We then talk with the child to see if his particular needs have been met with his parents. This gives us a program whereby we can work out the problems that triggered the acting-out behavior on the part of the child. If the parents are mature enough to accept their responsibility toward the child, and if they will continue in their new-found Christian life, we, under God, have success.

One day we sent a lad home and when he returned he was cursing his mother, who was crying. She left before we could talk with her. When the child stopped sobbing, he related the following story:

His mother had admitted that he was an illegitimate child. She had been promiscuous as a young girl and became pregnant by a soldier. The boy wanted to kill his mother.

When we got the boy quieted down, we read him the story of Jesus teaching from the tabernacle porch. The Pharisees had brought the woman taken in the very act of adultery. They wanted to follow the Mosaic Law and stone her to death. Jesus settled the problem by telling the one without sin to cast the first stone. We handed the boy a stone across the desk, told him to go home, and when he felt that he was without sin to hit his mother with the rock. That was several years ago, and last time we talked to the lad the stone was still in his dresser drawer. Christ handled a twentieth-century problem as easy as he did in the first century. Could this be coincidental?

One day we were called into the juvenile court and the judge committed a child to the Ranch for stealing. He had also been found eating out of garbage cans at local restaurants. When we arrived at the Ranch we heated him some baked beans with sugar and some wieners. He couldn't eat the food because it was too rich. He pointed to a can of black-eyed peas and ate that. You see, the child was eleven years and eleven months old, just one month away from his twelfth birthday, and he weighed twenty-seven pounds. Jesus Christ sent this child to one of His facilities where he would find the proper care, love, and nourishment. This happened twelve years ago. Just recently the young man, now weighing one hundred thirteen pounds, visited me one Sunday at the Ranch.

One of our current youngsters, whose father had abandoned his mother, noted a man in a black leather outfit riding down our road on his motorcycle. He ran out to the man, yelling that it was his daddy. I started down to check on the excitement, trying to preclude a kidnapping attempt, when my ex-Rancher related to me that he was now a karate expert and that he could protect me. He hurried on ahead to handle any problem that might arise. My eyes welled with tears when I thought of that twenty-seven-pound waif of twelve years ago. Jesus had used "His Ranch" to let that little guy grow into a caring young man.

We invite local civic clubs to the Ranch to eat a meal with the children. The kids adopt a member, eat with him, give him a tour after the meal and answer any questions that come up.

We had one youngster who had been praying for many days that his mother and dad might somehow get enough money to pay their house rent. It seemed as if they were going to be evicted and the lad was concerned about his family being put out into the street.

One day we invited our local Optimist Club out to lunch and the boy that had been praying about his family sat with the president of the club. After their tour they were standing in front of the administration building talking, when the Optimist said to the youngster, "Don't I know you? I've seen you somewhere, I know." The boy shook his head negatively. The man said, "Where do you live?" The boy answered and the man said, "Hey, I own that house." I heard the tail-end of the discussion and told the man the lad's problem. He immediately reduced the rent and forgave the back payments. The Lord Jesus worked the whole thing out. Is this just coincidence?

Another time we asked some engineers out to give us an estimate on a roadway we were praying about. One of the kids invited the men to have lunch with us. As they were eating, I noted that one boy and his guest stopped during the meal and bowed their heads as if in prayer. The boy later related that he had led the man to Christ during these few moments together.

Our children pray for all the Ranch's needs. They pray for our food each day and it is provided. The children know exactly where it comes from, too. They are allowed to eat all they want, but they must eat all they take. They must have a little of everything on the serving line.

One day as I was walking through the dining hall, little Beth was sitting at a table all by herself. As I passed by she looked at me and I noticed two large tears trickling down her cheeks. She was violently chewing, both jaws puffed out like a little squirrel, and she asked in such a pitiful voice, "Will you make these kids quit praying for broccoli?"

We have devotions every night and one night I was in the little boys' cottage, nine years old and younger. (We sometimes wonder just how much we say rubs off on the kids.) I found out this night because when we kneeled to pray, little Eddie next to me prayed, "Dear God, please be with all those who smoke. Every time they take a drag off a cigarette, the Holy Spirit goes - Cough, cough, cough."

In the early days of the Ranch, right after we began, we learned an awful lot about prayer and faith. God showed us in so many ways that He is a faithful God and that He would take care of us. I remember during the first few weeks out in Groveland two boys that got sick and had 102-degree temperatures. Rather than send them to school, we took them the local doctor in Groveland. He advised us to take them home, put them to bed, and give them some aspirin to reduce the fever. If they didn't get better he said to bring them back. On the way back to the Ranch we were troubled. We had been able to hire our first set of cottage parents and didn't have any pajamas for the kids. I thought about teenage boys laying around, in just their underwear. I was talking to God on the way back about getting some clothing and things for the kids. When we got back to the Ranch, I started to go in the dining room door. Two cardboard boxes were sitting there. I nudged them aside with my foot and took the kids in, fixed them something to eat, and put them to bed. I went out and got the boxes. I set them on the dining room table and opened them. The first box was full of girls' and women's clothing. I thought it was some kind of a joke, sending these out to the Boys' Ranch (at that time we had only boys), then I noticed a note which said to use these for rags. We certainly could use anything to help us keep the place clean, so I felt a little better. I opened the second box. Halfway down to the bottom was a pair of size fourteen pajamas that would just fit Roger. Down at the bottom of the box was a pair of yellow nylon shorty pajamas size twelve, that just fit Kim. We never did find out where the boxes came from.

During our first days in Groveland besides the rags to clean with, we needed some dustpans, brooms, and mops. We were very tempted to take money out of our meager petty cash account and purchase some supplies, but we prayed, and that day some ladies from town came and brought some boxes. In the boxes were a half-dozen metal dustpans, brooms, mops, and other supplies. We began to learn a little about faith. We needed some toothbrushes, toothpaste and soap to train the kids in proper hygiene. Again we were tempted to go buy them, but we prayed and remembered about the dustpans. That afternoon, the juvenile court chaplain came out and laid a sack on my desk. I let it sit there and finally he said, "Open the sack." I said, "Well, Preacher, I already know what's in the sack." He said "Okay, what's in the bag?" I told him, "Toothbrushes, toothpaste, and soap." He never did figure out how I knew.

We had a dog named "Bonn" who was a beautiful animal given to us by a couple who moved to Florida and couldn't keep the dog in their apartment. They were a "service" family and got the dog in Germany. He was a beautiful animal. He became sick at the Ranch and began to cough. We were in Groveland one day and we had him with us. We went by a veterinarian office and the boys said, "Let's take Bonn in and get him checked." We stopped and I explained to the vet that we didn't have any money but would he check our dog. He said he would be happy to. He found that Bonn had heartworms. He said the treatment would be between two and three hundred dollars. Back at the Ranch, Bonn didn't seem to be getting any better and the kids wanted to take him to the vet to get the treatment started. I said, "Boys, we don't have any money. You're going to have to pray for your puppy." In their devotions that night they began to pray for Bonn and he seemed to progressively get a little better. A couple of months after that we were back in Groveland and had Bonn with us. Just on impulse, we stopped to see the vet again. He checked Bonn and found that there wasn't any sign of heartworms in the dog. This is a disease peculiar to the tropics and the only way to cure it is with arsenic in small doses, but God saw fit to heal the kid's puppy. Just another example—is this coincidence?

I remember speaking before a Rotary group and telling them some of the miracles that had taken place at the Ranch, and how God answered prayer. At the end, when I usually have a question and answer period, a man stood up and said, "These things you are saying are just all coincidental." At that time, it seemed like the Lord gave me the following illustration that I could answer him with:

"Back in those days, before we started our school, our kids went to public school. Our elementary kids went to the Windermere School, our junior high kids went to the Pine Hills area and our senior high had to go to Ocoee High School. One day three of our little kids ran away from school. We were really concerned because never had any of our little kids run away, and we were really frightened for them. I was speaking that night and I normally wear a suit and tie. This time I was so concerned about the kids that I forgot to get dressed up, or that I even had the speech. I got to the Ranch and remembered then, as I looked at my calendar, that I had this talk. I had to go back home to get dressed. On the way home, about 2 P.M., I was driving along Pershing Avenue and praying about the kids. I looked up and facing me, coming down the other side of the street were three little, bedraggled, dirty, sleepy, hungry-looking kids. I pulled my truck to the side of the road, they got in and I took them home with me."

Coincidence? Here we were—how many roads are there in Orange County Florida? There are thousands of them. How many seconds, minutes and hours are in a day? How could it be that I would be at this exact spot to pick up our kids at that exact time. You see, it can't be coincidental—it has to be of Christ.

We lost our lease on the house in Groveland and we had to find another place to move. We got down on our knees and prayed and asked God if he wanted us to continue and where he wanted us to go? He touched the heart of a lady in Orange County who owned a one-hundred-sixteen-acre orange grove.

She agreed to give us seventeen acres on a ninety-nine-year lease for one dollar a year. This was the first debt we had ever incurred and we felt we might be able to pay a couple of years in advance. We were jubilant. We had to be off our campus by July of 1968, and this was about May or June of the same year. We looked for a place to move our kids into, however, we had no building for them. We prayed and one day I received a call from a local doctor at Holiday Hospital. He said he heard we had some land and didn't know if we were going to need any buildings or not, but he had a building across the street from the hospital which he was going to tear down and put up a professional office building. My wife and I went to look at it and it was just what we needed—a concrete block duplex with room for the cottage parents, on one side and a kitchen and dormitories on the other side with a bath on either side. We told the doctor we were tickled to death and it was an answer to prayer. Then we checked around and the cheapest bid to move it out on our property was $4,000.

Up to that time the biggest donation that we had ever received was $600, but we prayed and asked God to supply the money if He wanted us to have the house. One day I went to the mailbox and there was a letter from the Junior Sorosis of Orlando with a check for exactly $4,000. We were able to move the house out, set it on its foundation and get the kids moved in just at the same time we had to be out of the house in Groveland. I wonder if the house suddenly was going to be torn down, if this was just a coincidence, or if Christ had known about this all down though the ages, and at this point in time He would have the house there to take care of His kids at the Ranch?

When we had the land given to us, we were jubilant, however, we needed to get a zoning hearing. Since it was all agricultural, we needed to get a change in zoning so we could have a place for our children. The people across the lake had built some pretty expensive homes and they were concerned, and rightfully so, that someone would be building a prison camp for kids across the lake from them. They had raised some money and hired an attorney to fight us and keep us from getting the zoning change. We went before the Zoning and Planning Commission of Orange County and it was too emotional for them to handle—they referred it to the County Commission. We had our commission hearing and the chambers were completely full of people, and many others in the hallway. There were pros and cons and even an editorial in the local paper saying that we should not "push motherhood and apple pie" in order to take advantage of the neighborhood. There were questions that were legitimate and needed to be answered—that our children were not criminals but were young Christian kids. They certainly would be an asset to the community rather than a harm. I think over the years, as we look back, we can see that this actually happened. It really has become a great asset over the past twenty years. At any rate, I began to find out a bit about what it takes to be a politician. The County Commissioners at that time knew we were a very poor organization, that we just lived day-by-day. They put the following criteria in an agreement that if we met it, we could go ahead and get temporary zoning:

1. They said we couldn't use an existing well on the property that was 1,000 feet deep, had an eleven-inch casing, and a 100-hp motor big enough to take care of a whole community of people. Since no one had taken television pictures of it or kept a log on it, they didn't know whether there might be seepage in the pipes. We had to agree to put

in a new well at a cost of around six- or seven-thousand dollars.

2. Any building we did on our property had to have a floor level of 86 feet, and the ground level there was 83 feet. This would require a three-foot berm which would cost in excess of twenty-thousand dollars just in land preparations before we could even start building.
3. We would not be allowed to use septic tanks, so we had to put in our own sewer plant. Everyone in the agriculture area out there used septic tanks, but they were talking about a twenty-thousand dollar future expenditure that there was just no way in the world we could come up with.

So, everyone in the opposition had grins on their faces. They knew that there was no way in the world this could happen and we could ever meet these three conditions.

The commissioners felt good and were patting themselves on the back because they had taken care of both sides. They figured if we could do what they asked, this would be great. If not, they had given us a chance. So, we began to pray. A man in Tampa became interested in our program, for a sewer plant and through some of our board worked it out that they began to build it. We got our sewer plant built and paid for. Then a local road builder heard about the situation. He came out with his trucks and cut down the beach area, which incidentally or provincially, we discovered had sugar sand and now has a nice, white sand beach. He loaded this dirt, spread it, and compacted it with his trucks. He did the twenty-thousand-dollar job and forgot to send a bill. We had a man dig our well, and I remember when he reached about 350 feet, he told me they hit muck and not much use in going any further. Normally, once they reached muck they withdrew and started a hole somewhere else. But we told him that's where God intimated we were suppose to dig, and just keep on going. He continued down to about 550 feet, and we have what appears to be an inexhaustible supply of good, sweet water. Thus, all three of the conditions were met and we were able to continue building our facilities.

Many times we can see God's plan from years back as He looks down the future and uses His various facilities and ministries to take care of things. I recall that a grandmother brought two boys out for an interview. It seemed their mother was in a mental hospital in California and the father was an alcoholic. He had left the mother and brought the two kids from California back to Florida. He was picked up on a DUI charge and had to spent his weekends in jail. The two little boys had set their grandmother's mobile home on fire and she couldn't handle them. She didn't know what to do with them. She heard about the Ranch and came out to talk with us. We require that the parents be in our counseling session once a week and also be in church services. Since their daddy couldn't be there, the grandmother said she would work with us. Each night the two boys would pray about their mother. After they had received Christ, they learned that God answers prayer, and saw the prayers being answered for other kids, they began to pray that their mother could come back. Again, we didn't have any idea what the conditions of her confinement were, how long she had to stay, or anything about her situation. But we send our kids home one weekend a month, and this weekend their grandmother picked them up. This same weekend, my wife and I had gone to a retreat. We came back on Sunday afternoon as the parents were bringing the kids back. I noticed this strange lady on campus—a very nice looking young lady. I walked up to her and said, "May I help you?" She said, "Well, no, I'm here visiting my boys." I asked her who her boys were and found out that she was the mother of the two boys from California. She had been released from the mental institution and had come back to find her kids. That night we had our Sunday evening service and I asked her to stay for that. We had a Jewish man who had received Christ and he was preaching. His wife was a former member of the Jehovah's Witness sect. When I was talking to the woman earlier, I asked her if she was a Christian and she said she was studying to be one. I asked her with what denomination and she mentioned that she was studying to be a Jehovah's Witness. So this night was just a way that God had worked the whole thing out—she sat right next to the Jewish preacher's wife who had formerly been a Jehovah's Witness. At the end of the service when he gave the invitation, she very sweetly received Christ as her Savior and was helped quite a bit by the preacher's wife. I thought it might be a good idea if we kept her here at the Ranch and put her on our staff in a position where she could really learn to be a good Christian mother and take care of her kids. She agreed to this and we hired her.

Her former husband came back and tried to get her to go out with him. I'll never forget when she explained to him that she would not go out and stay in a motel with him. If he wanted to get her back, he would have to begin to treat her as a Christian lady. He would come out and take her to dinner and bring her back on campus by ten o'clock. He would bring her flowers and candy and began the courting process all over again. They were eventually remarried and took their children and left the Ranch. I'll never forget the boys—they said to the other kids,

"I told you Jesus would bring my mother back." The last time I heard from the man, he called and had joined a Pentecostal church. He evidently felt called into the ministry and had become a preacher. When he called, he was really giving me the plan of salvation over the telephone and trying to get me saved. But isn't it wonderful how Christ works through the lives of people and restructures families, if they simply have faith in Him? Certainly not coincidental, but Christ.

One day a young man, sixteen years old, came into my office with his mother. During the interview she indicated that he had traveled from New York City and had been getting his meals out of garbage cans. The police were concerned about him. He was from another county and she was trying to get him to come to the Ranch, since he had quit school. When they left for their tour, I noticed that he walked with a limp and I said, "What's the matter with your foot, son?" He said "Sir, it's not my foot—it's my leg. I was in an automobile accident in New York City and my leg was cut off above the knee." He was limping because the prosthetic device had never been replaced. He had stuffed towels between the stump of his leg and the prosthetic device to fill the gap in there, and it caused him to limp. When they came back from their tour we talked with them and decided to bring the boy out and work with him. At the Ranch, he still was having problems with his prosthetic device because it didn't fit him. He and his brothers in the cottage were praying about the situation and if we might be able to find some help. One day I got a call from an ex-Rancher who had been sent out to the Ranch for growing marijuana.

While he was at the Ranch his brother was in a motorcycle wreck and lost an arm. At any rate, the boy finished our program, went back to school, graduated from high school, went to college and graduated from the University of Florida. He came back to Orlando. When he called me, he asked that the kids pray for him. I asked him what was wrong, and he told me he had melanoma cancer on his chest. The doctor said it was something that could spread really fast. He said he was going to have surgery. I asked him if he had been going to church and praying. He said not as much as he should, but he knew God answers prayer and he asked us to please pray for him. I told him we would certainly do that and asked him to let me know what happened and to be in touch. He went in for surgery and when released he called me and said it was successful. They had done a beautiful job of plastic surgery to cover up the scar, and he wanted to come out and show it to me. I told him to come out, that it would please me very much. So he came out to the Ranch, and showed us the scar, and told me all about his business. It seemed that he had gone into a firm in Orlando that makes all the prosthetic devices that helped his brother. That is why he went back and got his education in this field. He asked if there was anything he could do for the Ranch. I couldn't help but grin at how the Lord Jesus worked all this out. I called the crippled boy over and introduced him to Paul, who was able to make him a leg for dress as well as a leg for all his athletics, and is still taking care of his prosthetic needs to the best of my knowledge.

Was it just coincidence that we attended a meeting of the Florida Group Child Care Association in Jacksonville Beach in 1980? At the meeting we attended (just to get a couple days away actually), it was brought out that the state minimum standards were to be changed. Several had to do with a policy that involved our faith ministry. One was that we would need to have a year's money on hand to purchase food. We felt this was in violation of our faith. We had begun the Ranch praying for our food day-by-day. At this time, we were praying it in week-by-week. If we had money in the bank for food, we wouldn't have to depend upon God to supply it.

Another rule they were attempting to promulgate was if a child was fourteen-years-old or older, he didn't have to go to church. If he was under fourteen, he could go to whatever church his parents chose. Since we were working with largely pagan families, this would have destroyed our ministry of requiring church attendance.

We began to essentially defy the Department of Health and Rehabilitative Service by refusing to apply for a child care license. Their rule stated that any dependent child held in care outside the family was subject to their jurisdiction.

It was our belief that only a judge could label a child delinquent or dependent. Since we did not work with adjudicated children, they were not dependent and thus were not under HRS rules. We, along with our attorney, went to Tallahassee on April 22, 1981, and met with the HRS attorney to explain our position. They would not accept this, so the cold war continued.

We knew that it was a hopeless fight to go through the court System. Rev. Lester Roloff, had tried in Texas, even up to a Supreme Court decision, and lost.

We decided that we would go to Tallahassee and attempt to get the law changed. In concert with another children's home in Tampa, we began. We soon had three other homes who joined with us.

We chartered the Florida Association of Christian Child Caring Agencies (FACCCA), as a peer accreditation association. We published by-laws and minimum standards which we felt met or exceeded those promulgated by the state HRS. We were fortunate in acquiring the best lobbyist, in our judgment, in the state of Florida; who, as a born-again Christian, gave his expertise, time and money to the association.

We began our lobbying effort—we appeared before various House and Senate committee meetings along with the Florida Group Child Care Association folks. We went through the humiliation of being referred to as "Elmer Gantry's" and as "child abusers" who wanted to practice child care in secret, by our opponents. Newspaper editorials and TV and radio interviews were held.

The following letter was sent out to all Senators dated June 2, 1980, by the Florida Group Child Care Association, Incorporated, by our opponents, and it said:

> "We need a stronger licensing law to:
>
> 1. Protect the health and safety and well-being of children in residential care
> 2. Establish child care and fiscal accountability.
> 3. Avoid commercialization and exploitation of children.
> 4. Insure permanency planning.
> 5. Prevent the haphazard establishment of residential child caring agencies by non-qualified persons.
> 6. Help prevent embarrassment to our state.

THE FOLLOWING CHURCH GROUPS AND OTHER ORGANIZATIONS SUPPORT THIS BILL AND MANY HAVE SPOKEN IN SUPPORT IN THE VARIOUS HOUSE AND SENATE COMMITTEES:

Florida Baptist Children's Home; United Methodist Children's Home; Church of Christ Christian Home and Bible School; Advent Christian Village; Assemblies of God Real Life Children's Ranch; Catholic Charities; Florida Sheriff's Youth Fund; Florida Center for Children and Youth; National Association of Social Workers; State Fire Marshall's Office; Group Child Care Consultants Services, Chapel Hill, NC; National Association of Homes for Children; US Children's Bureau, Washington, DC.

Your Support of this bill will be appreciated.

Sincerely

[The President]

The present law was to sunset in 1983 and the State Legislature decided to hold off a vote until 1984 with the hope that we could all get together and reconcile our differences.

We spent the year inviting members of the Legislature to our homes so that they could see for themselves how the children were being treated. We met with members of the group advocating licensing, which was the Florida Group Child Care Association, trying to work out our differences, but we couldn't work them out. The issue was then carried into the Legislature the following year.

On June 18, 1984, we received the following letter from our lawyer:

"This is regarding the successful efforts to have 'Registration' instead of 'Licensing' by the state of Florida for the Edgewood Boys Ranch and other Christian child caring agencies. On the last day of the Legislature, the House of Representatives, with only four dissenting votes, and the Senate, with no dissenting votes, passed the bill which will allow Edgewood and other Christian child care agencies to "Register" with, instead of being "licensed" by the state of Florida." In other words, we will be able to control our own organizations instead of being controlled by the state of Florida.

As you know, we were fighting this battle for over five years against what seemed to be insurmountable odds. In the beginning it was only Edgewood and one other Christian child care agency. At the end it was only Edgewood and some eight or nine other Christian child care agencies against, it seemed, everyone else. It was really US against THEM, and THEM included all of the major religious denominational children's homes.

It was truly a miracle that God brought about this final result. There is no other way that what happened could have happened, had not God placed certain dedicated Christians in the right places at the right times. The title of the bill passed is Senate Bill 230. We have been informed that Senate Bill 230 will be presented to the Governor today. The Governor has three options: sign the bill and it will become law immediately;

do nothing for fifteen days in which event the bill becomes a bill without his signature; or veto the bill. Although we do not anticipate the Governor to veto the bill, which includes changes in provisions other than those that pertain to us, your prayers that he will either sign the bill into law or let it become a law without his signature, are needed and will be appreciated. Although there were scores of people that worked directly in this cause, and I am sure countless hundreds and perhaps even thousands of Christians that prayed, wrote letters and called their legislators on our behalf, I would like to single out two of those dedicated Christians put by God in the right places at the right times. They are Dick Hollahan, a Lobbyist in Tallahassee, who coordinated and managed our efforts this year; and Representative Herb Morgan, from Tallahassee, who is the Chairman of the House Appropriations Committee. They should receive our special thanks. I can only say in closing that we should give God the Glory for the great thing He has done.

Governor Graham signed the bill, and we then were able to send out the following letter to all the different children's homes throughout the state of Florida. It goes as follows:

> "As a director of a home for dependent children, you and your Board of Directors have a choice on, or after October 1, 1984. This opportunity was created by the passage of committee substitute for Senate Bill 230 (CS/SB 230) in the last session of the Florida Legislature.
>
> CS/SB 230, now known as Florida Statute 409.170 established a 'Registration" concept for residential child caring agencies as an alternative to licensure by

> the Florida Department of Health and Rehabilitative Services.
>
> The Association is presently implementing the requirements of FS 409.170 and invite your inquiries concerning membership."

As a result of this letter, approximately seven other homes then joined the group that was getting registration rather than licensure. As an aside, the state had requested the rule that we be required to have money on hand to provide food for the children for one year. One day we received a call from a gentleman who wondered if we could use some dried food. I told him, "Yes, we don't turn down any food, and we would appreciate getting it." We went over to a warehouse where his son had been in business selling dried food. All this food needed was water to make it edible. They were selling it to a lot of people who had bomb shelters and were worried about hurricanes. They could put in units of food, enough to take care of a whole family, and store it in their garage. When we arrived there, we found that the young man who had the business had gotten married and didn't want to stay in this area any longer. The father had told him about Edgewood and he gave us his entire inventory of dried foods. There was enough dried food to feed the 60 or 70 kids we had at that time, for exactly one year. I couldn't help but look up and see God smiling down and saying that we didn't need the money—all you need is the faith; all you need to do is pray to me and I'll see that you're taken care of. I had the great joy of telling several of my friends in the HRS what had happened. Was it coincidence or the Lord Jesus Christ that had that taken place just at that time?

In 1984, along with seven or eight other families, my wife and I were helping set up and start a mission church in Anaheim, California. One of the other families that were assisting in this mission work was John and Donna Crean, and we became very good friends. We had left California, came back to Ohio and eventually down to Orlando to begin the Edgewood mission. We needed a mobile home out on the property which we had leased from a lady in Orlando and we called John and Donna to ask them if they ever donated anything like this. (They were in the mobile home manufacturing business.) They said, "Certainly." They made arrangements for us to go to Haines City and pick out a mobile home that we wanted. They purchased us a three-bedroom, two-bath, fully furnished, mobile home with central heat and air. It was brought to the property and set up on a permanent basis. Ruth and I were able to move into it. Several months after that, John and Donna came back from California and visited us. We were sitting in the living room talking and John said, "Do you know Dr. Robert Schuller?"

I said, "No, I don't know him."

John said, "Well, he has the *Hour of Power* program." I know my mother had talked about it because she had cable TV and she listened to Dr. Schuller on that program. We didn't have cable and I never heard him. John indicated that he was a very close friend and supporter of the *Hour of Power* program and also on Dr. Schuller's National Board of Directors. He asked me if we would like to go to California and appear on the show. They had several million that watched it each Sunday and it would be quite a great exposure. I grinned and said, "Sure, I'd like to do that," never thinking that the possibility even existed. But after John and Donna went back to California, I received a call from Dr. Schuller's administrative assistant and he made arrangements for us to go there and be on the *Hour of Power*. We were able to fly out and appear on Dr. Schuller's program. He told us he was coming back to Orlando that same week and that he would like to visit the Ranch. We were able to pick Dr. Schuller up at the airport the following Thursday, bring him out to Edgewood and introduce him to our kids and staff. What a great individual he is, and how gracious he was. He told us he had been given some land in Zellwood, which is fifteen to sixteen miles north of Orlando, and he was going to get a mission church built there, of his denomination. He said they were going to appoint Harold DeRoo, a schoolmate of his, as the pastor. He asked if I could help him get settled in the community and introduce him around. I said, "Sure, I would be happy to do that."

When Pastor DeRoo came, we met with him and were able to help in some small ways of getting the church going. One day he called me and said he had grandparents in the church, and they were worried to death about their grandson—he was doing a lot of things he shouldn't. I told him to have the grandparents call to set up an appointment. We met with the grandparents, the parents and the son and accepted him at the Ranch into our program. The boy received Christ as his Savior and the following week both of his parents prayed and asked Christ to come into their life and to take it over. The boy did well in our school and was released. He went back to finish high school and joined the service. While he was in the service he took an examination and rated so high on the exam that he was eligible to attend West Point if this was his desire.

I couldn't help but think that here, from 1967 to 1987, we had seen all these things happen. There were people saved, families got straightened out, and all this took place in the eyes of Christ over a period of twenty years.

In June of 1984 we were having a crisis at the Ranch. This was the year we were fighting with the state to try to get out from underneath the licensing law and be registered. It was June when the Legislature was meeting, and we were praying about that. We had been able to purchase the remaining 100 acres of the land from our benefactors who had given us our original grant. We had to borrow $250,000 to pay off this debt and purchase the land. The local bank had been very good in giving us the money, and told us we didn't have to pay any of the principal for the first year—just pay the interest each quarter. We had managed to pay the first quarter payment in March, but now in June we didn't have any money to make a payment. In addition, we were $30,000 in debt in various current bills that we had to pay. It really looked like Satan had begun to win the battle, but we prayed.

My wife suggested that we call John and Donna Crean and talk to them about some ways that we might be able to raise the $250,000. We called them and they told us to come out to their home in Laguna Beach. So we went out and arrived in Laguna Beach on a Sunday morning. We went to their home, then out to have brunch at a local restaurant. They told us they had been praying about it and had decided to give Edgewood their personal check for $250,000 to pay off the mortgage. I don't think our feet hit the ground for the next two weeks—we were so pleased and happy that they were able to do this. We wired the check overnight mail, had it put into the bank, and the $250,000 loan paid. When we got back to Orlando we were hit with the fact that we had to get $30,000 some way. The Dr. Phillips foundation came out and talked with us and said they knew we were in a "tight" situation. They had been so supportive of us in the past, and said would give us $30,000, if the board would agree to match it. The board immediately decided that somehow they would match this $30,000. The agreement was made and we got the money from Dr. Phillips, which got us out of this immediate need. Then, as mentioned before, we got a call from our attorney on June 18 saying that the bill had passed the Legislature and was simply waiting on the governor's signature, which was finally forthcoming and we were able to get our registration bill. Here, in one month, a $250,000 note, $30,000 in everyday bills and a miracle in the Legislature. This all came about because of the direct and divine interference of Jesus Christ and no way in the world could it be considered as coincidental.

The Edgewood Children's Ranch, this year, saved the taxpayers of Orange County Florida approximately $3,000,000.00.

Edgewood Ranch is one of the points of light referred to by President George Bush. Not one cent of tax monies was used to care for the ninety-two boys and girls now domiciled here.

Would it be simply a coincidence if every county in the United States were to establish a like facility? Or, could we find people who would call upon and trust our Lord Jesus to provide?

It is an interesting thought!

CHAPTER THREE
RANCH PETS

Lucifer

We had a pet turkey that the kids aptly named "Lucifer." He did everything he could to merit that name. He hated me but loved the kids. The story behind "Lucifer was:

It was approaching Thanksgiving and the kids were home to celebrate with their parents. I had gone to my residence in Orlando in order to attend my home church. Before my wife and I left for church, the telephone rang and a man asked me if I'd like to have a twenty-seven-pound turkey. I told him that the kids would really appreciate it and assumed that he would deliver it to the ranch. Imagine my surprise when I returned from church to find a twenty-seven-pound live turkey tied up to my clothesline in the back yard.

He was very unhappy and was letting all my neighbors know of his displeasure. His "hate" for me began when I squeezed him in the cab of my pickup truck for a thirty-mile trip to the Ranch. He flopped around, hitting me with his wings and trying to nail me with his sharp beak, which he did on occasion. After avoiding several wrecks and being cursed by irate drivers narrowly missing my vehicle as I fought off the turkey, I arrived at the Ranch.

The boys fell in love with the turkey and laughingly called him "Lucifer." I agreed that he was named appropriately. He loved the kids, and if a turkey could smile, I'd swear that he smiled at the children while at the same time glared menacingly at me.

We take calisthenics first thing in the morning. Lucifer arose with his boys, and lined up with them while they did their exercise. I'll always have the mental image of that turkey trying to do "Jumping Jacks" with the kids. In an ungainly "hop" all the while slapping his wings, he imitated the exercise.

After breakfast the children walked about a mile down a lane to the highway where they caught a bus to take them to school. Lucifer always went along to see that nothing happened to his buddies. He would try to get on the bus with them but the bus driver wouldn't let him. So I had to pick him up in my arms and carry him, swacking and beating me with his wings, scratching with his claws and pecking any place I left an opening.

As I released him at the cottage, I looked around hoping to see a coyote or some sort of egg-sucking dog that might be looking for a turkey dinner. No such luck.

When the boys returned from school Lucifer was right there to greet his family.

Lucifer finally died. The turkey dinner was never an option. This was the only time in history anything named "Lucifer" ever got a Christian burial. As he was interned, a hymn was sung and prayers said. A cross was then placed over the grave to complete the ceremony.

Henry and Henrietta

Our brother and sister pigs who became part owners of the Ranch, were named Henry and Henrietta. They had access to the buildings, as well as the yard. No pen for these pigs—they were special.

It was hilarious to see the kids giving these pigs a bath in the lake, to try to rid them of their funky odor. Immediately upon their release, they would head for the nearest sandpile or mudhole and roll to get back to their natural element. The kids would scratch their heads and wonder how they could ever keep these pet pigs clean.

Bonn (our dog) would simply walk by and shake his head. He knew that keeping a pig clean was a hopeless task. The boys soon learned this also.

We taught a lesson here: the children were new Christians. They didn't have to return to their old way of life. Unlike the pigs, they had been granted new life in Jesus. So they tried to get Henry and Henrietta saved.

Article in Local Paper

A pig had been confined in a tight-fitting box by its owner.

The Orlando Humane Society took custody of the pig. After several weeks of care the pig was announced ready for adoption. The pig had been enclosed—nailed shut—in the box for almost a year.

The Edgewood kids adopted the pig and began to shower her with love and tender care. She was allowed to go wherever she wanted to whenever she wanted to.

She grew and grew until she was so big that she couldn't move. When she died, she was buried on the spot and she went from earth heaven to hog heaven. The kids cherish "freedom" for all of God's creation. Several years later the Orlando Humane Society had another abused pig that been mistreated—so they called the Ranch. They said that people "weren't exactly lining up at the door" to adopt a pig.

Six boys, along with their cottage "Dad," went to check out their new pig. They thought that they would be picking up a little "piglet" and was surprised to see that it weighed one hundred twenty-five pounds.

The sight of four full-grown men trying to lift a pig into their pickup truck made the kids wonder how they would be able to handle it. The pig let forth an opera of porcine music, dug in his heels and fought the four grown men. As soon as he was in the truck, miraculously the squealing stopped.

The boys climbed in with the pig and commented, "Oooh, he needs a Kleenex," "Oooh, he's so hairy," "Oooh, he pooped, but he looks like a nice pig. Will he eat in the dining room with us, Dad?"

The boys began to love on their new pig. They scratched his ears, and ran their fingers through his bristles. The pig was now quiet and content. He knew that he now had a family that truly loved him.

Buddy

The children raised a baby "bull" into a full-grown animal. They didn't believe the adage that "you couldn't fully tame a bull" and Buddy was the Ranch pet.

As he aged he grew cantankerous and began to show his true nature. We felt that it might be time to put him out to pasture, so we gave him to a local deputy sheriff who has some cattle.

The day the new owner arrived, he tied Buddy to the back of his pickup truck, thinking to walk him several hundred yards to a horse trailer he had parked. Buddy showed his unwillingness to leave his Ranch family. He butted the back of the pickup until it was clearly dented.

The kids cried as they watched their "Buddy" finally towed away.

The children had horses, sheep, goats, chickens, pet swine, turkeys and any other animal or bird that had been mistreated or unwanted.

Their capacity for love was unlimited. Many of them identified with the abused animals and their love changed the personality of the creature. We have seen homesick little boys hugging a puppy to their chest, while crying their little hearts out. The puppy would look up and lick their tears, in full understanding and with total empathy.

Animals are essential to rehabilitation.

Forty Registered "Poodles"

The Humane Society had found a kennel where the dogs were not being properly cared for. Guess what? They called the Ranch.

As the Director, always in need of money, I had visions of selling these "registered" dogs for enough money to ease our financial crunch. There were forty poodles. Some were large, some regular size and some were miniature. I learned my lesson. As long as we were taking abused animals as pets, we were blessed. But to take them for mere monetary reasons didn't work.

Can you imagine forty yelping, barking, howling dogs, all encaged in an area of chicken wire. To keep them clean and fed was a full time job and could they eat? They ate more than the kids, and we were soon praying hard for more dog food.

We tried to sell the dogs but didn't find a single buyer, so we began to give them away. After weeks of caring for these forty poodles, we finally gave the last one away.

This was the end of our commercial dealings with animals.

CHAPTER FOUR
CHILDREN'S TESTIMONIES

Rancher Testimonies

I believe the only reason I am not in jail is because Judge Arthur Yergy committed me to Edgewood Boys Ranch when I was fifteen years old. Although I had broken minor laws on several occasions I wasn't really a criminal. Judge Yergy realized this. He also was aware of something about me of which I didn't know. I could likely become a real criminal, if something wasn't done to change my attitude toward life. My poor attitude was caused, in part, by my parents divorce, and our living conditions afterward. However, most of this attitude was my own creation. Shortly after the divorce, I learned to make people feel sorry for me, then, it was easy for me to take advantage.

I didn't admit to myself that I felt I deserved more attention from everyone, than the average person. Because of the unusual hardships placed upon me by my parents divorce, I felt everyone owed me something. When things weren't going my way, I blamed everyone around me, but never myself.

When I learned I was to be sent to the Boy's Ranch, I was furious. I hadn't heard much about the Ranch before then; so I felt everyone involved in my placement at Edgewood did not understand me, or my feelings. I was wrong about everything! I expected a religious, juvenile home. I envisioned religious fanatics, bent on converting me by force. When I arrived at the Ranch, I was surprised to see everyone smiling. After I unpacked and made my bed, the first thing I did was to go swimming in the lake. Everyone seemed to be having a wonderful time.

After dinner, the boys and staff met in the living room. There was an informal question and answer period, in which I did much of the answering. We discussed the rules, written and unwritten, and I got honest answers to all of my questions. Then we had an informal devotion service. Each boy prayed aloud, and quite a few of them prayed for me. This seemed unusual to me, because I had grown up in a church in which most of the prayers were written in the Common Book of Prayers. Praying, to me, wasn't personal. To me, praying meant reading the same words, over and over again. I couldn't relate to the meaning of the words.

After the service, we went to bed. Everything seemed different from what I had expected. I was confused. In my first week, I learned I wasn't going to be punished for past wrong doings. The only punishment at the Ranch was for infractions of Ranch rules, committed after arrival there. There were no bars, no locked doors, and no fences! Everyone knew that he could run away, but getting caught meant being sent to the Florida Training

School. Everyone knew the State Training School was a place where brutal beatings and sexual perversion were common. The only training to be received there was criminal training. We all knew boys our own ages, who had been sent there. Many boys were sent to the state school for truancy, minor theft or vandalism. On many occasions these boys came home with the new knowledge of picking locks, "hot wiring" of cars, obtaining liquor, or sniffing glue. The only people for a boy in a juvenile home or training school to look up to are the older, more experienced boys.

At Edgewood Boys Ranch, the boys have Mr. John Lynd. Mr. Lynd is the world's best father. His most important contribution to the Ranch is love. He loves every boy there. Most boys don't understand how a stranger can love them, when they believe, and in some cases it's true, that their own parents don't love them. Most boys at the Ranch learn the reason. The reason is Christ. At first, many of the boys don't understand the motivation of staff at the Ranch, who work longer and harder than anyone they have ever seen. They soon learn that the motivation comes from Christ.

The boys at Edgewood observe the almost superhuman accomplishments of people like Mr. Lynd, Joan Consoliver, and the rest of the Ranch staff. They become a recipient of the almost superhuman love of people like Aunt Minnie Rouse. Each boy is given a better example of how to live than he could find anywhere else. Each sees the daily miracles that keep the Ranch functioning, and enable it to grow at such a rapid rate.

At the Ranch, I learned that the world owed me nothing. I realized that most of my actions before I went to the Ranch, were caused by ignorance and selfishness. The Boy's Ranch did not change me. It showed me a better way to live. I learned that my values had been confused. The staff at Edgewood set an almost perfect example of the right way to live. Each staff member shared the rewards that came from living the right way, with each boy there. We could see that they were happy with their lives. No one at the Ranch said, "Do this, or else." They said "If you do this, you will cause this to be the result." I learned that though I could get by, living off another's sympathy for me, I would do better, and feel happier, by helping others. I learned to show some initiative.

When I was eighteen years old I married a girl with similar ideals. We now have a three-year-old son, of whom we are very proud. I have a full time job and I attend Jr. College classes at night. My wife does a wonderful job keeping our house and she works full time. We aren't perfect. There are many things we should do that we don't do. We have imperfections which slow us down considerably. But because of the guidance I received, during and after my stay at the Ranch, and because of the occasional material help we have received from the Ranch, my family and I are headed toward the goals which we have set for ourselves.

Edgewood Boys Ranch didn't change my life. This can't be done for anyone, except through Christ. A boy can be shown the right way to live. Show him the great rewards of a good life by sharing these rewards with him. The process of sharing and responsible privilege is going on right now.

If you believe, as I do, the Edgewood Boys Ranch's method of handling the problem of juvenile delinquency is the best and the only really effective method, then you must agree that supporting the Ranch is a good investment for anyone living in the next generation. Support of the Ranch prevents a potential criminal from full development, a protection for his potential victims. "An ounce of prevention is worth a pound of cure." Each dollar spent now could save thousands later.

Edgewood Boys Ranch is an example to the world. It is successful. Your contributions and prayers will assure its continued success. When Edgewood Boys Ranch has proven to everyone that its method is the way to contain juvenile delinquency, others will follow the example and the problem will be eliminated. This problem is complex, but the answer is simple. The format is available to any who heed.

If you have money to invest in Edgewood Boys Ranch, please do so. But most important, whether you can help financially of not, remember the Ranch in your prayers.

A Rancher

MORE TESTIMONIES

We, as parents, have made mistakes, also, and we are working on those, too. We will have a good life together one day, with the help of God and the Ranch.

I love you,

Mother

How I feel the way Keith has changed. All I can say is that Keith was everything that I know he could be while he was home on Christmas vacation.

Now I hope our home will be good enough for him to want to stay. All I know is that we will try, and pray, that God will work our problems our from now on.

Sincerely,

Mother

Since Ernie stay there I have noticed a big change in him. He listens and is much more obedient. He seems to get along with people much better. If you could let him come home, we can make a much better home for him now than he had before. I think we are more capable of disciplining him in the manner that a twelve year old boy should be.

Thank you very much for what you all have already done for him and for myself.

Mother

Today after nine months at the Ranch, we feel that Denny is an entirely different boy, he has taken an interest in his school work, he is not belligerent in his attitude and he gets along will with people an in general a much better adjusted boy.

We feel that with the progress Denny has made at the Ranch and with our experience of getting along with Denny at home on his off-campus visits that Denny is now ready to come home with us permently.

Signed Mother and Father

Before we came to the Ranch, our family was in utter despair, and Jack most of all was suffering. When I decided to give my son back to our Heavenly Father, that was when the miracles of His love started working. Praise the Lord for His mysterious ways.

I can't begin to tell you enough how forever grateful I will be to the Ranch for giving us a second chance with our child. God sure is good and this being a time of Thanksgiving, I wanted to let you know how we appreciate all your love and support to not only Jack, but my husband and myself. What a wonderful blessing we have received. The Ranch has blessed our marriage and has answered my prayers.

Thanks for the smile on my son's face! Mother

The Ranch helped me to have a better understanding with my family and I learned to take my problems to

God. Its helped my mom to realize that she needs the Lord and that he can help her.

Since I've been at the Ranch my respect for elders grew more and more and I respected them. And I've learned how to pray. Many miracles have been while I was here for me an dif I had gone to the state training school I would never have been able to learn about God.

My love for things grew and I have a soft heart. I never thought a place could be filled with so many blessings until I came to E.B.R.

I just want to say I am grateful for what you have done for me and I love the staff and the Ranch for everything.

Kim

The following is a letter from the first girl accepted into our "Home for Unwed Mothers"

One of the produces moments of my life was at the hospital, when her son was born, to lift him up in dedication to our Lord Jesus Christ.

He was adopted by a solid Christian family.

Mr. Lynd

You suggested to me that I write my thoughts about my future career, down on a piece of paper. Well I can give it my best shot. Here it is first of all. I'd like to finish my last 2 years of high school. I'd like to go to a private school if possible. I think I should try to take some kind of course having to do with children. The more experience I have working with children the easier it might be for me to get a job working with them in the future. While I'm in high school, if I could get transportation, or could find a place close enough to walk or ride a bike. I'd like to get a job at a daycare center or nursery school after school. I could baby sit for extra money, also I really like kids. People say that I do really well with them. Once I get out of high school I of course, want to go to college, preferably a Christian one. The first thing I want to do is get a Bachelor of Arts degree or Teaching degree. Maybe later I'll go back to go a little higher. Who knows maybe I'll even get a Doctors degree. My goal is to be a kindergarten teacher. It probably will change by the time I get there but, it may not. The other main goal I have is to find a nice Christian man to marry. That's one of the reasons I want to go to a Christian college. That is my career goal. I'd also like to stay as close to my mama as possible.

Sue

A Day In The Life of a Girl Rancher

"Good morning girls," a too-joyful voice calls. Too joyful for 6:00 A.M., that is. Its Aunt Laurie (our house mother) calling us to rise and shine. Sleepily, I pull myself from the warm bed, dress and get ready for a new day. After a morning run around the Ranch, it's off to breakfast. Afterwards, I begin the chore I will have for the next two weeks, cleaning the bathrooms. I try to do my best on my chores because here comes Aunt Laurie with the white glove test.

Next, we have morning devotions with the cottage where we study our Bible memory verses for the month. Two days a week we go to chapel for praise and an inspirational talk, sometimes by a guest.

At 8:30 we're off to school. On the way we stop at the rose garden where we have a flag ceremony and pledge allegiance to the flag, which we do again at 5:00 P.M. as the flag is lowered. For God and Country is a big motto at the Ranch.

I hurriedly join my teacher, Aunt Barbara, as we walk to the classroom. At my desk, I look at my goal card, and decide I need to work in math. Before I realize it, it's already 11:15, time for lunch. Great, I need a break from e = mc squared. Pizza today.

After lunch, it's back to school work. On Tuesdays at 2:00 we go to choir practice, which is my favorite elective. I have so much fun singing, I hardly realize it is 4:00 and time to return to my cottage for afternoon work detail. Today I get to try my hand at landscaping (well, actually, I'm just raking). After work detail it's time to get cleaned up for supper. On Wednesdays we have physical education, softball and volleyball mainly.

Tonight it's our cottage's turn to serve dinner to the rest of the Ranch. After dinner, we go to the playground or to the rec. center for free time. On Tuesdays, we eat an hour earlier so we can get to chapel. Here we hear leaders from all over Central Florida give testimony to God's power at work in their lives; people like a Delta pilot. Chief Wilson of the OPD and two of his majors, a major from the Sheriff's Department, a stock broker, pro football player, housewife, doctor, lawyer, and ditch digger. It really strengthens our faith to hear these people share their faith and their temptations and failures. This makes it easier to accept our own imperfections while always striving for personal improvement.

After an hour of recreation, it's back to the cottage for showers. Now comes a special time of the day, evening devotions and prayers. After the Lord's Prayer it's lights out at 9:00 and off to bed. Aunt Laurie makes her rounds, giving us hugs as she says to each of us, "Sweet dreams, I'll see you in the morning." I hear soft music in the background as I drift off to sleep. Lord, it's been a good day. Thanks be to God.

A Girl Rancher

CHAPTER FIVE
PARENTS' TESTIMONIES

August 14, 1967

Mr. John Lynd
Edgewood Boys Ranch Foundation
P.O. Box 8181
Orlando, Florida

Dear Mr. Lynd:

It has been our pleasure since returning home from our trip to have Tom at home with us.

He has exhibited a spirit of cooperation and steadfastness that has made both his mother and I and his sisters most happy. It is my belief that he has also enjoyed this prolonged visit as much as possible for anyone.

Tom shows a heightened sense of unity with the family and a cheerfulness of disposition that has been entirely lacking for the past several years. He has been cooperative in all things at home and has shown a real will to enter into family life.

He has expressed the feeling that for him to get ahead and for him to maintain the place in life he should have, that it is necessary that he apply himself strenuously to school work. Doing his assignments with a will. I believe his determination to be genuine. We encourage and assist him in this effort.

If you believe him ready to return home, we are most happy to have him resume his place in the family.

It should be added that Tom took the initiative in getting the paperwork started to re-enroll in Robert E. Lee, Jr. High in the hope that he will be permitted to return to the family.

Sincerely,

[His father]

August 14, 1967

Dear Dr. Lynd:

Although it may not be necessary to add my personal thanks to Tom's letter, I feel that I must do so. Having our son home these past few weeks has been a pleasure I would never have suspected to have again only a short year ago.

From someone who seemed to be a stranger—and an unwelcome one—our son has returned to us!!! A year ago, our whole family was tense, upset and distraught that it was only by sheer will power that we stayed together. All over our son's behavior. I simply could not understand Tom, his father's attitude toward him or my attitude toward him. In fact, it was almost to the point that I was afraid to be at home alone with him. I am certain that Tom's pa could not understand my attitude.

Since Tom has been home this time, however, his dad has taken time out to be with him so very much—taking him with him every time he could and even allowing him to stay in the office sometimes. In all ways, the two of them seem to be much closer and what more could a mother ask for? They seem to have a better understanding of each other and a closeness that is completely new.

Tom's attitude toward me has also changed. He no longer lets me have those sulky, mean, sneaky looks that were so disturbing. Instead, he teases me out of my anger (when my Irish shows up) and gives out to all of us a great deal of emotion and affection. He's fun for all of us.

As for me—who knows themselves well enough to judge? I HOPE I have managed to change my attitude. Seeing my two men getting along—even if it means standing against me—is what I have longed for. At any rate, Tom seems capable to managing me to my satisfaction. What could be better?

Again my many, many thanks for all you have done for all of us and especially for Tom—I personally feel that you have given him a chance for life. Let's hope and pray that every boy you have may change as much as he has.

Yours sincerely,
His Mother

Through the combined and invaluable effort of the dedicated Ranch staff and our Pastor, John has been remolded into a helpful, charming young man with a surprisingly mature understanding of his own problems and weaknesses plus a true Christian compassion for the frailties and failings in others.

Night and day are no more different than the boy who entered Ranch and the young man who returned home two weeks ago. (This startlingly different young man who now appreciates our home and is taking pride in improving our lawn and garden.)

This past week has been an excellent test for I have had to work overtime, yet have returned to an orderly house, a cheerful greeting and offers to fix me something to eat. Also, virtually every night he has shown me something he has repaired or has tried to return to working order. The very fact that, on his own, he located and talked with his former principal, to make sure he could re-enter Robinwood Jr. High is virtually a miracle in view of his previous attitude on school and his history of truancy.

We have "discovered" a Church and Pastor we mutually respect, enjoy and trust. We have needed this for many years. We now have a new inner strength and feeling of security because of it. We are now assured help and understanding is available when we are confused and distressed. (No man is an island.)

The enormous change in John's attitude and his open acceptance of Christ and His Church is apparent to everyone.

Very truly yours
His Mother

The change in Bill is unbelievable. We brought—you a sullen, uncooperative boy who had no purpose in life. You are returning to us a cheerful, willing young man with positive goals in life.

Mother

Since Ronald has been at the Ranch he has become more respectful and obedient to us and willingly helps with the necessary work around the house—often asking if there was something he could do before being asked. Ronald now seems to want to go to Church because it is a Church and not just Sunday and he always remembers to give his tithe.

He now asks if he can go out and always returns at the time specified—no roaming around. He has become more self-sufficient and accepts responsibility (which he refused in the past). This was very noticeable during Christmas when his mother was in the hospital and I was working. He did as he was supposed to without "Goofing" off.

Sincerely yours
Signed His Father

The Ranch has done many things for our son. He has been given self-confidence, taught how to respect and to be respected. He has learned more self-control, self-adjustment, judgment of other people and himself. He has made decisions, followed routines and schedules and carried out orders.

Mother and Father

What the ranch has done for Billy and his family? It has made Billy a fine young man who does work and volunteers for work and doesn't mind getting dirty and does his best to get his job done. He takes pride in his appearance and read and worship God and doesn't demand anything. He has learned much in the Bible and not ashamed to be a Christian. I am proud and honored to be his mother. He loves his home and keeps his room and drawers neatly. We pray together and worship as one in Christ. We know God works miracles as we have seen one happen in our own family with Ed. I am proud and honored to be a part of Gods ranch. Billy, has led one young boy to go back to Church and not be ashamed to say he know Christ.

Yours in Christ
His Mother
6/2/77

P.S. Mary has learned to love and be loved, Pray that our daughter Kitten will see that the only way is to believe in God and put Him first.

Dear Mr. Lynd

This is to inform you that we desire Jonathan to be released on June 15, 1984, as we feel his progress has been excellent and nothing more would be accomplished by delaying this return home.

We wish to gratefully thank you and each staff person who contributed and to the wonderful changes we have seen take place in our son during the past 6 months. Significant positive attitudes toward himself and others have been noted as well as an increased awareness of who God is and what our relationship to Him should be. Also, the fact that he seems to recognize right from wrong and wants to choose to do the right thing is another positive development we've noticed. Academically his grade average has maintained in the high 90's and we feel confident that he can compete on his grade level now.

We praise God for this home-life that has been provided by your ministry, as we feel it was an answer to our prayers. We are thankful for everything that has been done to help assure Jonathan's Christian maturity is reached as well as his social maturity. We are proud of your effort and especially proud of Jonathan's results. We hope to continue to stay in touch with you in the future, and be of assistance if needed. May God continue to grant you success in your outreach ministry through the coming years.

Sincerely in Christ
His Mother and Father

To all those at Edgewood who were there to help us when we needed it most.

We're together again as a family and as friends because Edgewood was there to help us bridge the gap between us.

Thank you!
Mother

I will never be able to repay you and all the rest of the staff have done for Robbie and me too, but will try with all my heart to get it paid. I ask God every night to help me and all of you there.

A Mother

Thank you for the miracle of helping us and giving our son, Jerry, a new lease on life.

If I never believed in miracles before—I believe in them now. Your dedication to assisting families is most inspiring. I would never lose faith in mankind now that I have seen firsthand all that is possible. Our hearts are full of joy and appreciation.

Signed
a Mother and Father

CHAPTER SIX

PROMINENT PEOPLE'S TESTIMONIES

Excepts From Prominent People on File

The character of the child is molded to the strengths that built our country—patriotism, independence, love of God and our fellow man, to be respectful of self and others—these are Edgewood's contribution to our community.

What more could we ask?

Bill Morris CLU,CHFC

It is significant that formal education at E.C.R. has been of the highest quality, furnished in addition to all other aspects of the ministry for the children and parents.

George R. Overly, PhD
Chancellor Freedom University

The facility as it stands, the reputation that the Ranch carries, but most importantly of all, the family lives that have been changed are a living testament to the dedication of the ministry.

Harold De Roo, Pastor

The savings to the community is inestimable. To think of these beautiful children ending up in prison—what a loss. We might note that it costs $25,000 a year to keep a person in prison. All too often those in prison, their children go to prison as well.

Donald S. Brown D.V.M.

I am confident that the economic impact of Edgewood on the community is positive from the standpoint of keeping many people from being put on our tax rolls in a form of jail, mental health rehabilitation, etc. The families that I have seen put back together and grow through the love and understanding and teaching of Jesus Christ through this organization are numerous.

Steven F. Foremen, Business Leader

On the occasions that I have had to visit at the Edgewood Children's Ranch, I have been amazed at what outstanding work you are doing in our community. Your program has benefited so many children and their respective families and I wanted to take this opportunity to thank you.

Danny Wilson, Chief of Police
Orlando Police Department

Your lessons of ethics and patriotism, of duty to God and Country, and of determination and belief in oneself are all vital to the success of the youngster, for whom you care and whose lives you enrich.

I commend you for your attention to the oft-forgotten "basics" to teaching and practicing "old fashion manners," and for maintaining your facility in such a way that one-on-one instruction may continue to be provided for the individual as necessary. While you at the Ranch state that the "typical Edgewood child is a child for where life comes without a safety net," I am confident that most Edgewood Children upon departure from the Ranch, deeply believed they have indeed been blessed with a safety net, that net is Edgewood Ranch.

Bill McCollum, member of Congress;
now Attorney General of Florida

As a legislator in the Florida House of Representatives and particularly as Chairman of the General Government Appropriations Subcommittee, I all to often see wonderful programs that we are unable to fund with taxpayer dollars. You have shown that it can be done without government funds and the inevitable attached strings, yours is an example that deserves to be followed.

Fran Carlton, State Representative

Edgewood Children's Ranch has a wonderful story to tell. Without a single dollar of taxpayer money, you have accepted troubled children, placed them in a caring, situational environment and involved their families in a program to help these young people get their lives back on a productive track.

You are a tremendous asset to Orlando and a model for communities across the country.

Bill Frederick, Mayor of Orlando

The Edgewood Children's Ranch is an outstanding example of what can be accomplished with faith, prayer, and a lot of hard work. The principle under which you operate and instill in the young people entrusted into your care have changed the lives of many children and adults. The Ranch has provided and alternative to juveniles who could have impacted our jail and court system at considerable cost to our taxpayers.

Vera M. Carter,
County Commissioner Dist. 1

This letter written to share some of my personal reflections regarding the services of Edgewood Children's Ranch, which I believe has been so successful over the years because of its Christian philosophy and emphasis on the involvement of and restructuring of the family in your work with the children.

I have always been impressed by the love and caring shown by you and your staff toward the children and their love and caring shown to you in return. That all of this takes place in a disciplined atmosphere is truly commendable.

Rayetta R. Beaver, Agency Relations Director
United Way—Orange, Osceola
and Seminole Counties

Although I have seen several such undertakings, I have never seen one so well managed. I have some idea of the difficulty of managing youngsters of varying ages. You and your associates have done a marvelous job judged by the immaculate condition of the buildings and equipment and the conduct of the boys and girls enjoying such privilege. I have never seen its equal.

U.S. Ambassador, Retired
Rotary of Winter Park West, Orlando Florida

If you missed the meeting last week (held at the Edgewood Ranch) you missed a thrill that is hard to put into words. The enthusiasm of youngsters far less fortunate than any of us, from homes far less than anything like any of ours is indescribable. Their brightness is infectious. You can't help but get excited about raising money for them when you see the tremendous work going on there by the staff. It's tough to forget the warm clasp of an 11-year-olds hand as he looks up and says "Hi! I'm Brian. Who are you? You're my guest. Would you like to take the tour?" "This is where I sleep—this is my closet, I clean this bathroom." It goes on, in an endless stream of the zest of a young man gaining confidence for the first time in his life.

Seeing that for the first time that he doesn't have to be (as he admits) a bad kid to have people love, respect and like him. I walked away from the Edgewood Ranch last Monday morning a better person just from being there, talking to the kids, seeing what its like and trying to figure out how I can help, just knowing that the Ranch's program is working. The funny part about that is—I want to see if I can help them. It was the best program we ever had—and the only thing that can top that is having breakfast out there and presenting them with a check for $10,000 no better cause.

The Rotary Club sponsored the "Archie Campbell Edgewood Benefit" to raise the $10,000.

Archie visited and spent several hours at the Ranch, where he fellowshipped with the children, who all fell in love with him.

One little fellow who, after asking Archie if "He was a Christian," and receiving a very positive answer in the affirmative then asked, "Why do you smoke those cigars?" Archie answered in his unique way, "Son, I have to do something to keep from being perfect." The little guy seemed satisfied with the answer.

Dr. Jim Lynd, Counselor at the Ranch
Brother of Jack Lynd

"Dr. Jim" was noted nationally for his expertise in detention. He developed the Orange County Detention Home and Parental Home into modern nationally recognized facilities with an adjoining Court House.

The original detention home was composed of a small reception room, and cells for white boys, black boys, white girls and black girls.

The parental Home was all crammed into one building when he took over.

Jim's statement:

I guess I'm like Jonah. The Lord told me in 1969 to come out here. I wouldn't go—I didn't see how the Ranch could work. I mean, they had no budget here—they were never sure of a payroll. My faith wasn't strong enough to believe. So I went my own way, fighting the call to come here. I had poor health almost this whole time of fighting God—two open-heart surgeries, and a collapsed lung. Now I'm here at the ranch and healthier than I've ever been. This is where I'm supposed to be. The Lord gives you peace when you're in His will.

My thinking has really changed. I think I always believed, but this is more real. Christ is becoming personal and practical. I'm living those things that I only believed were true before.

In all my work I've never seen anything to compare with this Ranch. The biggest miracle is how they do it. I doubt if Jack ever knows where the money's coming from. They pray for absolutely everything they need. And they just trust the Lord to provide it. They do not owe a dime to anyone—all the buildings are paid for. They trust on a daily basis for operating expenses. People send in $5. or $10., or someone dies and leaves money in a will. It just comes in. They don't get ahead. They just stay even day to day.

And then, too, there's the miracle of how they reach the kids. I've studied psychology—there must be 230 schools of sychology—none agree. Most are useless in really reaching the heart of a child's problem. Freud, for example, says man's not responsible for his own actions. Christ says he is. And I have learned that the only key to changed behavior is in Christ's teaching when He says that to change you must have My Spirit.

The Ranch tries to reunite the family. The family is out of tune with God, and as a result the child is out of tune with life. The children come here confused about lines of authority. If they have not seen their parents as authority figures, they will get their education from their peers, and they will get into trouble. If they are sent to a state training school, 75% of them will get into further trouble. It is because there is no work with the family, the source of the real problem.

Our first priority in counseling parents of troubled children here at the Ranch is to get them to admit that there is a problem. Then they have to realize that in their own power they are incapable of solving it. Our counseling is a Biblical kind of problem-solving. We advise that if you will pray about something, God will show you His plan in this, and through Christ you can work it out. No problem is unsolvable with Christ.

We try to teach the children here not to be afraid to love. Many of them are afraid of being hurt and cannot show love. After they've been here for awhile, they come up to you and hug you, and they mean it. This is the greatest thing—to learn how to love—to trust enough to be able to love. And this is what the ranch tries to give the children through Jesus Christ.

CHAPTER SEVEN

BITS AND PIECES

Hush Puppies by Charlie Wadsworth

Orlando Sentinel

Jack Powell was so impressed by the desire of the Edgewood Boys Ranch lads to aid another boy in need of help this week that he decided to do something about it. And in so doing he received a surprise that impressed him even more, and made him doubly determined to do something about it.

The Edgewood boys voted to give a newly acquired tricycle to Eddie Kirkland, a young cerebral palsy victim whose own three-wheeler was stolen last week. Eddie needs a special bike like the three-wheel job for transportation to pursue his sale of health foods. Powell wanted to start a fund to buy another three-wheel bike and give it to the Edgewood boys. Here is where the second surprise entered the picture.

"We're grateful, naturally," said Edgewood director Jack Lynd. "But the boys know that when they give something to someone that it is their decision and they do not expect anything in return except perhaps thanks. We teach them how good it is to give. And if you could have seen their faces when they voted to give the bike to Eddie you would have been caught up in that spirit.

"Gifts come from their hearts," Lynd added.

Letters

In the establishment of a Children's Ranch, it is necessary to make literally hundreds of informative talks in the community. It is necessary to get people to visit the physical facility to see and feel what is taking place. One of those talks remains rather vivid in our mind. It happened soon after the opening of the Ranch.

The following notice appeared on the bulletin board of the University Club:

Announcement Card: Oct 1, 1966

Nov 4, Friday 3:00 P.M. John W. Lynd, Director Edgewood Boys Ranch. "New concepts in the prevention and cure of Juvenile delinquency"

Chairman

I received this letter on Sept 26, 1964 subsequently.

Dear Mr. Lynd

I just woke up in the middle of the night with the thought that your "new approach" in the training of boys might be a religious one. Your brochure emphasis that aspect. We had a speaker in August who was supposed to tell us of the curative value of chlorophyll, but he said, that of course "God does the healing." That was not exactly news to us. The speaker had promised it *would not be a religious talk.*

I was naturally concerned when we received this letter. All I had to talk about was the wonderful ways that our Lord Jesus answered our prayers and changed lives for the better. I was filled with apprehension as we approached the speech. Those men all had doctorates and believed in freedom of thought.

We told of miracles of answered prayer and the Christian philosophy of our program. Afterwards, as the men left the building and shook our hand we heard remarks such as, "This took me back to my childhood when I went to Sunday School," and other such comments.

Nov 7, 1965, We received the following letter:

My dear Lynd:

We want to thank you for the fine presentation, the treatment of your problem at the School. The response of your audience showed the appreciation of your visit and what you are doing for unfortunate boys.

We want to thank you, again, for coming to us.

Cordially,
Signed,
Chairman Program Committee

O ye of little faith. All the concern was wasted. Our Lord Jesus had those who needed the witness in a place where they heard the power of prayer, that He answered from the mouths of His new, little converts at the Ranch.

"Celebration of Halloween"

Our kids went door to door on October 31, 1975 and passed out tracks. (Became an annual custom)

They also handed the following letter to each recipient.

> October 31, 1975
> Dear Friends:
>
> We are from the Edgewood Ranch in Orlando, Florida. We are not taught to believe in witches and goblins. However, we do believe in the supernatural: that Christ and His Angels and Satan and His Angels occupy the spirit world. We feel that children who destroy property are working with Satan and his angels. As we are on the side of God and His Angels, we want to do something good for you.
>
> Because you have supported the Ranch, we have received all of our material needs; so instead of taking or asking any treat from you, we would like to share with you the greatest gift the world has ever known, that of Jesus Christ.
>
> Please read the attached booklet and it will tell you how you can have this gift. By allowing us to share this gift with you, you have given us the greatest "treat" a child could have.
>
> May God Bless you.
> Sincerely yours

Arnold Palmer signing autographs.

One day, as I sat in my office in a meeting with our Social Worker and Chaplain, we were interrupted by a school teacher leading a disruptive student into my office. She stated, "This boy will not do his school work; he totally ignores us when asked to do something. He just has that 'dead' look in his eyes. We want him removed from the school."

I told the lad to sit down across the desk from me and asked him, "What's the problem, Paul?" He was sitting with his head bowed and when I asked him the question, he looked up at me. His eyes were hypnotic and I couldn't remove my gaze from him. I thought to myself, "Why can't I blink my eyes?" It seemed like the eye contact lasted for several minutes. This I saw a scene that I will never forget; gyrating figures doing, what to my mind, were Satanic dances and worship.

I was finally able to break the eye contact and said to Paul, "Rock music, huh!" He nodded in the affirmative.

I later asked those in the room how long I had stared into Paul's eyes. They said just a few seconds. (There is no time in eternity.)

We counseled with Paul. He prayed and asked Jesus to forgive him and remove the evil from him. After returning from his next weekend leave he brought all his tapes and we had a nice bonfire. I mentally saw "demons" rising with the smoke. Hard rock music is the tool of Satan and is the ruination of many a young person.

They listen to a tape over and over until they can play it in their mind any time. These tapes tell the child to disobey teachers and parents, as well as many other negative thoughts.

Ice Cream

The Orlando area was used as a "sampling" area for new products. After the sample was completed, and the popularity of the item could be estimated, the remainder was pulled from the market and given to a local non-profit organization.

We have an iron-clad rule against the children chewing gum. In the Tropics, it causes havoc when disposed of on a sidewalk under the mercy of the Sun, or placed on a school desk, or in the cafeteria.

Imagine my surprise one day, entering the dining hall, and seeing the kids all looking at me, grinning, and chewing away.

The market had been testing "Bubble Gum ice cream" and had sent the residue of the sample to our kids.

Children in front of the McGuire Cottage.

My immediate thought was that the kids had gone over my head and prayed to the "Holy Spirit" who sent them their chewing gum.

Jesus' Birthday Party

We try to teach our children that it is better to give than to receive. Each year, at Christmas, we have a "Jesus Birthday Party" where we have a cake with "Happy Birthday Jesus" on it. We have the cake with ice cream, then sing happy birthday to Him.

We then go to the Chapel where each child gives his/her birthday present to Jesus and explains why they are giving Him this particular present. They have wrapped it and now place it under the Christmas tree.

It is customary that they pray for several months prior to Christmas about exactly what is most precious to them that they can give to Jesus. All the gifts to Jesus will then be given to needy children in a children's home in Mexico, or to some really deprived children elsewhere.

Our children learn how God, our Heavenly Father, gave His most beloved Son as a gift to them out of His love for them.

I remember when John came to the Ranch. He was a big, strong 15-year-old, and was street tough. He had a little stuffed animal that he took to bed with him each night. It was dirty and smelly, but was his security blanket.

At first the other boys in his cottage made fun of him but after a few fistic encounters they accepted him and his little stuffed animal.

On the night of "Jesus Birthday Party" he gave his stuffed animal to Jesus. It was his most prized possession.

Twin Boys

We had twin boys that came to live with us. Their mother had muscular dystrophy and was confined to a wheelchair. Their dad was losing patience with her, and there was discord in the family.

One of the twins, Dan, had always wanted a good camera. His ambition was to be a photographer. He would walk around the campus and envision a particular scene. He would take a "pretend" snapshot for his mental album.

One day, totally unexpected, his dad brought out an expensive Nikon camera. Dan was jubilant and while he couldn't afford film, he took dry shots wherever he went. He loved his camera.

On Jesus' party, he tearfully gave his camera to Jesus. Those of us in attendance shed tears at this self-sacrificing act. With his

The Edgewood Choir.

family in discord, and no hope of getting another camera, he gave his most prized possession to Jesus.

Note: "This was one gift we set aside and gave back to him when he was discharged."

A little girl, whose Mother had died, left her with a small gold locket. This was the only material reminder she had of her mother. She gave the locket to Jesus.

Other children who had nothing, gave "themselves" to Jesus and some of them still serve Him, in ministry or missionary work.

The Optimist Club of Orlando gave the children a sum of money to buy Christmas presents. They had just a little money to buy gifts for mom, dad, sister, brother or friend, but the majority of them bought something for Jesus first.

A local department store opened their doors early for all our ninety kids to shop. It is a heartfelt experience to see such unselfish buying by kids that had very little for themselves.

They had learned the great lesson: "It is better to give than to receive."

Multiply these gifts by the hundreds that have been given to Jesus by the Edgewood kids, then realize the thousands of gifts they have received back from Him. You cannot out-give Jesus!!

Three days before the Annual Awards Banquet, scheduled for June 18, 1984, Edgewood Ranch experienced another tremendous blessing. The father of one of the children came to visit his son at the Ranch. Due to a divorce, he had not spent much time with his son in the recent past and found him to be drastically changed. Impressed, the father asked what had been responsible for the transition. The son explained that he had given his life to Jesus Christ and that it was Jesus who had made all the difference. After initial disbelief and confusion, the father listened intently as his son gave his testimony. In a few solemn moments, with heads bowed in prayer, that child peacefully and joyfully led his father to a new life in Jesus Christ.

Other Answers to Prayer

When we first opened the Ranch, we had a water pump that ran continuously 24-hours a day. All the experts we had look at the pump inferred that it couldn't possible run another 24 hours. Some three (3) months later, a member of our Board of Trustees secured a new pump and the day they brought it out to install, the old pump quit.

One day the Ranch foreman and I were talking about getting some day-old bread and how we might go about it. In the middle of our conversation the telephone rang and a lady from

The Edgewood Choir with the gift of new robes.

Powers Drive Baptist Church said to me, "Mr. Lynd, you have been on my heart all night. What can I do to help you out there?" I jokingly said, "You don't happen to know anyone in the bread business?" She said yes, my next door neighbor. The next day and from then on we had day-old bread.

I talked with Alan Travis, our CPA, on the telephone one day about our need for a copy machine. People were writing in from all over the U.S. asking for copies of our unique Christian Charter and other information. He advised me to check with some of the companies to see how reasonably we might purchase one. I agreed, and hung up the telephone. Before I could take my hand away from it, it rang back and a woman said "Mr. Lynd, can you folks use a Veri-fax copy machine our there?"

We were leasing a Ford Econoline truck which was our only Ranch vehicle and the one I used to make pick-ups in Orange

County and to commute back and forth to Groveland. One day I got concerned about what would happen at the Ranch if a boy hurt his back or got snake bitten and needed to be conveyed to the hospital. I took the vehicle to the Groveland Ranch site and gave the keys to the Ranch foreman. I told him to take me back into Orlando and that I would walk until God saw to it to give us transportation for this phase of the operation. On the way back into town, we traveled the old Winter Garden Road and stopped by John Roger's used cars to thank him for a $25.00 check he had sent to us. He handed me the keys to a 1957 Ford Ranch Wagon.

During a severe drought during the spring of 1967, we asked the boys to pray for rain. It rained just on the Ranch and nowhere else. Then we asked them to pray so everyone, might get rain, and within three days the drought was broken.

One of our new employees, on the first night she was on the grounds, put her contact lens in a cup before she went to bed. The next morning her husband got up and either drank them or poured them down the drain. At this time, Jean was in her forties and had worn glasses since she was 8-years-old. (The kids prayed about their Aunt Jean's problem). Two weeks later she went to her optometrist and upon examining her eyes, told her that she now has 20-20 vision and that she no longer needed glasses.

One day the Cottage couple went to Top Value Redemption Center to get a power mower. The lady at the center indicated that they were a book of stamps shy. As they were standing there debating what to do, a little old lady approached them and asked them if the lawn mower was for the Boys Ranch. When they nodded yes, she laid her only book of stamps on the counter and with a big smile on her face, walked out the door.

Feeding the horses.

Can you imagine on a pensioners income how long it took that little old lady to save a whole book of stamps, and how she might have long yearned for some little item that she gave up in order to help the kids get a lawn mower.

I spoke one night at the Good Shepherd Catholic Church in Azalea Park. Preceding me on the program was a lady who made an appeal for the Catholic Charities Home for Unwed Mothers. She asked for a set of dishes and for some linens. Knowing that we had two sets of dishes and that we taught our boys to share, I offered her a set of our dishes. That Saturday she came to pick the dishes up at the office and approximately two hours later, I got a call from a member of our Board of Trustees, who said a Catholic lady, totally unrelated to the Azalea Park Church on the north end of the county had called him and demanded that we accept dishes for our boys ranch. They were much finer than the ones we gave away. Here is God, replacing our gift almost before we can share our blessing.

During the Christmas season, 1967, we were notified by the Salvation Army that our boys were to be considered as recipients of new shoes from the shoe fund. It was indicated, however, that there were many more needy children then they had shoes to give. When our boys were told of this condition, they immediately declined the offer of new shoes and offered to share the shoes they had with the Salvation Army.

Tom Wenig, Pastor of Edgewood Baptist Church and founding father of Edgewood Boy's Ranch had been called to Iowa to be at the deathbed of his mother, who had been opened up and found to be full of cancer, closed up and the children were called to be with her in the end. The kids started to pray and by the time Tom got to his mother's bedside, she had been miraculously cured.

We had another boy assigned to the Ranch, who was one of the biggest problems in Polk County. We feel that it must have been with a chuckle that the Polk County Judge assigned this boy to the miracle-working ranch. The boy caused trouble from the first day, and had to be repeatedly chastised, both in a punitive fashion as well as having visits and other privileges removed. He even had to be locked up one weekend in the Juvenile Home in Orange County. This young man's problems seem to stem from a father who was habitually drunk. When

Children in front of the rose garden at Edgewood Ranch.

the boy was placed on extended leave, preparatory to discharge, he and his family visited relatives in North Carolina. At this time he made arrangements to be Baptized in a little country church. He had a talk with his father, who at this juncture accepted Christ as his Savior and was also baptized to the amazement of all, especially the family. They are definitely a law-abiding Christian family now living in Polk County. This has to be described as a Miracle of God.

Another employee was hired in January, 1968, who had been in a terrible accident, which involved a shattered heel and ankle, removal of half of his left kneecap and a broken arm, which was broken in three places and dislocated at a 90-degree angle. Casts were placed on both legs and a sling on his arm. The Doctor told him that it would be a minimum of 6 months before he could go to work again and maybe longer. Within

6 weeks of the accident he had both casts removed and was walking without the aid of crutches.

One of our first boys was a 16-year-old lad named Ralph, who had left his home and was living with two other adults. He was picked up for cashing bogus checks. He, along with all the other 6 siblings, left the home prior to their 16th birthday due to the brutality of a drunken father. Within 5 months of the time of his acceptance by the Ranch, the father had quit drinking and all the siblings has returned back to visit with the mother and father. The father used to get up early on Sunday morning and come out to the Boys Ranch before daybreak and take his son fishing. Ralph was released to his parents and was then hired back by the Ranch to work as an assistant counselor, while he continued his education. Two week after he was back a the Ranch in the capacity of counselor, his father shot his mother in the head and then turning the gun on himself, blew the back of his head off.

We immediately released Ralph to return home and live with his parents. On the 3rd day his mother was pronounced out of danger and released from the hospital. The bullet had entered her temple and discharged over her left eye without causing any permanent or serious damage. The father lay in critical condition, hovering between life and death. It was then they discovered that his drinking had been caused by pressure on the brain caused by a steel plate that had been placed in the back of his head due to an injury received as a soldier in World War II. The man was eventually released back to his home. He was nothing more than a vegetable, paralyzed, who could do nothing for himself. Ralph cared for his father during the entire convalescent period until such time that the man was able to care for himself. Faith and Prayer and the goodness of God was all that laid between this man and woman and death.

George was assigned to the Ranch and we never got any visits from his parents. We tried to contact the parents and seemed to miss them at every opportunity. One day the parents came to the Ranch in Groveland and asked me what they could do to help their son. I explained to them that in my opinion, they should take him home on visits. The boy suffered from extreme anxiety over the apparent lack of concern of his parents and as a probable result suffered from enuresis. The parents told me at this time that they had taken the child to a psychiatrist before he was placed at the Ranch. The psychiatrist had indicated that George was an arsonist and a sex fiend. They told the couple that if George was left at home with their twin baby daughters, he would probably attack them sexually and if he was frightened in any way, would probably kill them. This information was unknown to us prior to the time that we took him in at the Ranch. It was for this reason the parents did not have him at home. We then explained that George took his regular turn at burning the trash and that he was exposed with kids in the dorm. If abnormal sex was his desire, we never noticed any abnormal misbehavior during the time that he had been with us. We suggested that we still felt the best thing for George was that he be taken home. When they decided to take him home for a trial visit, the boy became so excited he actually wet his pants. The father had recently been discharged from the Air Force. During the last 6 months of his tour of duty, the mother had been attempting to sell their home so they could move to Miami where the father had employment after his discharge. Up to this time, there had been no person in a 6-month period who had come to look at their house. That night when they all got home, and they watched how George picked up the twin babies, they decided they had made a horrible mistake. That night they decided to become a whole family again and ask for George to return home. The next day a woman walked into their house and paid them cash for it.

CHAPTER EIGHT

PRE-ADMISSION STUDIES "TYPE OF CHILD SERVED"

PRE-ADMISSION STUDIES

Robert

PROBLEM

Robert has been in Educational Handicapped classes for 3 years. He is short-tempered, impatient with his work, and seems to have a bad attitude about doing school work. His parents have tried to get him in private schools but they won't take him because of EH placement needs. They have taken him to a doctor, but haven't put him on medication yet. They were referred to us by their doctor. He is capable, but doesn't apply himself. Robert admitted that he is the problem and started to cry during the interview.

FAMILY BACKGROUND;

The family consists of both natural parents and Robert. He is an only child. The parents told us that because of their demanding careers, they realized they did not have much time to devote to a family and had no more children. The Father is a former police officer who faced many negative and upsetting problems while "on the street." He admitted that he just couldn't face the problems of parenting and let his wife be both mother and father. She is a computer operator who works nights. They have worked opposite shifts for years and now realize what problems this has caused for the family. There has not been enough supervision in the home. She is now trying to get better hours and he no longer works for the police force. He has started his own electrical business and tries to work with his son in it.

NOTES

The family is from Ft. Myers. She is from Minnesota originally, of German origin. She is Lutheran, he is Baptist. She seemed unfamiliar with what we meant by "synod." All three prayed to receive Christ. We gave them an application.

Signed, Social Worker

PRE-ADMISSION

Tammy

PROBLEM

The social worker describes her as "out of control." She has been in "all kinds" of trouble and has seen the "Greenhouse" counselors in Kissimmee. She is a bully, fights in school, and destroys things. She has physically hurt her younger sister, and one of her older sisters is afraid of her. She lies and steals money from her sisters. She has failed 3rd grade in spite of average intelligence. She has torn their front door off the hinges and has destroyed the tool shed.

FAMILY BACKGROUND

The mother has been divorced from the natural father about 3 years and has been remarried about 1 year. There are 2 older sisters, ages 11 and 13, and a little sister age 4. The mother feels her father is a bad influence; he taught her to fight and helped destroy the mother's authority. Once Tammy got mad at her stepfather and said she hated him and wanted to kill him.

NOTES

Both prayed to receive Christ and Tammy said she wanted to come. We gave them an application. The mother admitted to using a belt on her for punishment. We noticed welts and marks on her legs and thighs. Her clothes were dirty. She seemed to have that "haunted" look in her eyes and seemed unusually thrilled when Mr. Lynd gave her a "birthday ring."

Signed, Social Worker

PRE-ADMISSION STUDY
James

PROBLEM

Jim was released from the Ft. Lauderdale Hospital psychiatric ward for the interview. He was placed there for behavior problems, which were severe enough to cause his mother to be hospitalized for stress. Jim reportedly has an I.Q. of 120 but has failed the eighth grade. He wants to "do his own thing." He has broken every rule his parents give him, stayed out of the home for days, and seems very angry at something. His mother commented that she and Jim have similar personalities; they will "keep things inside" until they explode in some way. She reportedly has ulcers and is diabetic, which are both aggravated by stress. Jim has seen counselors for several years and has attended military school. The controlled environment helped him, but was too expensive. The psychiatrists and the HRS worker recommended a boarding situation. Jim's problems seem to have begun when he was about 2 and was told that he was adopted.

FAMILY BACKGROUND

The family consists of mother, father, Jim and an 18-year-old natural son. They seem of the upper middle class in society; they were well-dressed, spoke proper English, and drove a Cadillac. They seemed to be unusually proud of their church connections, of the people they knew, and of the church offices they have held. From the look on Jim's face, I have a feeling some of the problems may stem from his disillusionment with their "Churchianity." They waited until the very end before they mentioned that Jim is adopted. "By the way, I'm sure this won't make any difference, but..." Then we got a glimpse of how they had spent years making sure it hadn't made a difference, and how they'd told him repeatedly how "lucky" he was to have been adopted by them.

Signed, Social Worker

PRE-ADMISSION STUDY
Paul

PROBLEM

Paul's natural parents are divorced. He has lived with his mother until a year ago and now lives with his father and stepmother. They work most of the time and seem very busy with their careers; he is working to establish his own business and she is in real estate. Paul has an I.Q. of 122 but has been having academic difficulty and cannot behave in school. He has been in public and private schools and tested by several agencies. They were referred to us by HRS. He does not qualify for military school because of behavior. The records they brought seemed to indicate that Paul feels guilty regarding his parents' divorce and rejection from his new environment. He seeks TLC from his stepmother and doesn't get it. According to the reports they brought, there was NO INDICATION OF ANY SEVERE OR CHRONIC EMOTIONAL DISTURBANCE.

FAMILY BACKGROUND

The father and stepmother live in Sarasota. They represented an upper-class socioeconomic level of society. She wore fashionable pants and a low-cut blouse. She also wore a large diamond ring. He was tall, slim, and dark. He said he is "building a new young enterprise" and tried to "make a deal" with us about Sunday visitation; he didn't want to "waste" his time driving up here when he could be working and "making you people more money." We didn't give in and he finally sarcastically said he would fly up in an airplane if he had to. We told him that would be fine.

NOTES

They hedged on the question of Christianity. We gave them an application.

Signed, Social Worker

PRE-ADMISSION STUDY
Mark

PROBLEM

Mark is an "A" student making E's. He has been tested and found to have an I.Q. in the "high average" range. He has been involved in taking the keys and going into neighbors homes uninvited. The parents were referred to us by teachers and counselors at school. They have had counseling by the mental health clinic and have seen a doctor. Mark is reportedly a sufferer of low blood sugar and is on a special diet.

FAMILY BACKGROUND

Mark is an only child, seems very polite and says he likes sports. He has brown eyes and black hair. His natural parents are divorced; his mother is white and has remarried a black man. Mark's natural father is in the Marine Corps in Kansas City and presently will move to Washington, D.C. He reportedly is trying to have Mark for the summer, which the mother doesn't feel is wise. The father seems to be trying to buy Mark's affection by spending lots of money of him and letting him do what he wants. The mother said that his father and stepmother don't make him follow his special diet, for example, and let him spend the days at a mall, going from movie to movie or whatever he wants to do.

NOTES

The stepfather is a pastor of a Holiness Church. He and the Pastor at Edgewood had many friends in common. Both parents were Christians and Mark had accepted the Lord. Mark said he wanted to come and we gave them an application. They seemed very cooperative and pleasant.

Signed, Social Worker

PRE-ADMISSION STUDY
Cassie

PROBLEM

The Father reports the problem as being "way behind in school." She was evidently born with a cleft palate and the original surgery was done incorrectly. She recently had corrective surgery which left her with a lisp and a nasal voice. She has a bad attitude, low self-esteem, and a hot temper. She doesn't obey her mother and has made low grades (below C's) in spite of average intelligence. They have had numerous conferences with the school, all to no avail. The father said they were so pleased with her brother's progress that they wanted Cassie to have the same program. At first, the mother wasn't in favor of it, but now she has changed her mind.

FAMILY BACKGROUND

The family has 2 other children at home; the son at Edgewood Ranch and another girl aged 6. Cassie complains of being the "middle" child and getting left out. Cassie now says she does not want to come to the Ranch. The brother thinks she will not get along with the cottage parents. We gave them an application.

Signed, Social worker

PRE-ADMISSION STUDY
Joey

PROBLEM

The parents described the problem as "extreme disobedience." Joey has a bad temper and often reacts violently when told to do something he doesn't want to do. He will use bad language and yell obscene comments when someone makes him angry. His behavior record at school is bad. He does not keep up with his studies. The police have been called on him twice. He has no court record yet. Joey is a quiet, shy-looking young man who doesn't look capable of such actions. He has brown hair and eyes, and a slight build.

FAMILY BACKGROUND

The family consists of Joey's natural parents and a natural sister, age 14. There are two older sisters from the mother's first marriage, ages 16 and 15. The family lives in the area. The father is a food transporter and the mother does office work for a sales organization.

NOTES

They all claimed to be Christians. They were referred here by a teacher. We gave them an application and a clothing list.

Signed, Social Worker

PRE-ADMISSION STUDY
Kevin

PROBLEM

Kevin has a learning disability (dyslexia) and a slight lisp. He has been in a private school for 4 years and has considerable trouble with reading. He is large for his age and freckle-faced. His parents were referred to us by a teacher at the school and a doctor, who recommended a highly structured atmosphere away from the family. There seemed to be family trauma associated with family counseling. Kevin has been on 3 prescriptions: 2 uppers and 1 downer, which did not seem to please his mother. His mother reported that the doctor said Kevin's system was "out of balance" and that made him moody. His mother feels that Kevin has become bored and just quit trying. His mother says he is strong-willed, bull-headed, and wants to make his own decisions. They have considered a military school. Kevin wants to be a professional baseball player; he thinks he doesn't need an education for that. He apparently needs to develop peer relationships, since he has been separated from his age group because of his learning disability. Kevin has been given stomach relaxers for a stomach problem which has been diagnosed as emotionally related. He reportedly has a "ulcer temperament."

FAMILY BACKGROUND

The family consists of both natural parents and one 17-year-old sister. The father works at the Space Center and the mother works at a bank.

NOTES

Kevin seemed lethargic about coming to the Ranch, but he realizes the family has had a long, hard struggle and they all need a release. Kevin talked about church easily. He has attended youth activities at his church. All 3 prayed to receive Christ, and we gave them an application.

Signed, Social Worker

PRE-ADMISSION STUDIES

James has regressed this year academically, socially and emotionally. This was his first year at our school and he experienced rejection and humiliation from the other students. They made fun of his very dark skin and often teased him about his dirty and shabby clothing. He had been deeply wounded by these verbal assaults.

Since January 1982 James has been staying out all night, and sometimes is missing for 2 to 4 days in a row. Numerous parents have called and notified us that James shows up at all hours of the night. Often he has not eaten supper. He wants to play with their child and sometimes begs to spend the night. The police and H.R.S. have been notified of this problem but have given no assistance to the child or the parent.

This past month James has become a serious behavior problem at school; highly disruptive, moody, hits other children, throws things, and refuses to do his work. He has become increasingly resistant and hostile and appears very sad, bitter and discouraged. There does not appear to be a strong bond between James and his mother.

This child desperately needs to feel loved and accepted in a Christian environment. He needs to have some success experiences and to grow and understand that he is very special in God's eye and that God has a plan for his life.

Signed School Guidance Counselor

James was accepted at the Ranch. I remember looking out on the recreation field and seeing James throw a football 50 yards. (He was eleven-years-old).

He identified with my son, who encouraged him to study and prepare for college. He returned to the community, enrolled in High School, and received a football scholarship. To this day, he stays in contact with my son and is doing well.

PROCEDURE FOR ADMISSION OF A CHILD TO EDGEWOOD CHILDREN'S RANCH

1. The referring agency, family, or individual will first ask that the Edgewood Children's Ranch consider the child for possible placement at the Ranch. The contact should be made first through the Executive director.

2. The Admissions Committee (consisting of the Director of Social Service, Director of Community Service, Executive Director, and one layman from the Board of Trustees) will then begin the process to determine whether the child shall be placed at the Ranch. The admissions process shall be as follows:

A. The child's family, social, and school history, including any psychological or psychiatric evaluation, shall be submitted at the time of application, including medical and dental reports on the child.

B. The Admissions Committee of the foundation will meet once each week to determine the eligibility of the referral. This meeting will be held on Mondays at 3:30 P.M.

C. The parents or guardians, and if possible the child, shall be interviewed by the entire committee. This interview will help to determine the parents' attitude, potential and willingness to accept appropriate guidance and counsel all during the time their child is at the Ranch. The purpose of this is that the family shall be in the process of rehabilitation and the working through of their problems at the same time that their child is in the process of rehabilitation and the working through of the child's problems while at the Ranch. Any information omitted in "A" above will be obtained at this time.

D. If the child is incarcerated, he shall be interviewed by at least one member of the Committee. This interview shall determine something of the child's attitude, potential and possibility of adjustment at the Ranch setting.

E. The committee shall, then come to a determination as to whether the Ranch will accept the responsibility of the child and their family.

F. The appropriate agency or family will then be notified of the Committee's decision.

G. No further action will be taken by the Ranch on the case until a proper written legal referral order has been obtained from the judge or the Juvenile court having jurisdiction, together with a written report of the medical examination of the child.

H. The Director of Community Services will then conduct an investigation into the child's home, school and church. He will determine weak areas that might concern the child's problem. He will meet with the Pastor or Priest and follow through on the family's church attendance and participation.

My special thanks to my wife Marty for her encouragement and hours spent on the computer interpreting my incomprehensible writing, editing, correcting, etc.

Edgewoodchildrensranch.org
407-295-2464 Office Phone